THE QUIET OPERATOR

THE QUIET OPERATOR

Special Forces Signaller Extraordinary

by
JOHN SIMPSON

with
Mark Adkin

The Story of Major L. R. D. Willmott MM, BEM,
Croix de Guerre, Netherlands Bronze Lion,
Netherlands Resistance Cross.

LEO COOPER
LONDON

First published in Great Britain in 1993 by
LEO COOPER
190 Shaftesbury Avenue, London WC2H 8JL
an imprint of
Pen & Sword Books Ltd
47 Church Street, Barnsley, South Yorkshire S70 2AS

ISBN 0 85052 376 1

Typeset by CentraCet, Cambridge
Printed by Redwood Books,
Trowbridge, Wilts.

CONTENTS

MAPS

FOREWORD

by

Colonel the Hon C. M. Woodhouse, DSO, OBE

One of the benefits of surviving for almost half a century after the Second
World War is that I am continually learning new facts about our wartime
operations and my own wartime companions. No doubt this process of
education will go on for the rest of my life. For example, I had Len Willmott
under my command more or less for about two and a half years, but most of
what I know about him today comes from this fascinating book by John
Simpson.

The two-and-a-half years in 1941–43 during which our lives overlapped
fell into two distinct phases. The first was in a training establishment for the
Special Operations Executive on Mount Carmel, where I was chief instructor
and Len was a W/T instructor. To call myself chief instructor is something
of an exaggeration, for the school was divided into two separate wings, some
distance apart: one was for general training in weapons, explosives, unarmed
combat and so on, and the other for radio operators. I lived in the former
wing and had general charge of the training programmes, but the W/T wing
managed itself, so I had only occasional contact with the radio operators.

One thing that was plain to me about most of the W/T trainees was that
they wanted active operational service, not just to sit in the background
tapping keys. This was true of none of them more obviously than Len, who
already had years of service as a boy soldier. When our team was picked for
the first major operation of SOE in Greece — the attack on the Gorgopotamos
railway viaduct — we needed men who could adapt themselves to any
hazards, not just the operation of W/T equipment. As a matter of fact, for
several weeks our W/T sets simply did not work, so our operators spent
much of their time handling explosives instead. This was just what Len
wanted.

One of his colleagues from the training school, Doug Phillips, had the
extraordinary experience in Greece of parachuting by night straight into an
enemy garrison town. He was immediately gathered up by friendly towns-
men, who hid him for several days while the enemy searched for him, until
it became safe to smuggle him out to join the rest of our party. Sadly, as Len
himself tells it, Doug was later killed on active operations. This was a painful

reminder that W/T operators were indispensable, and in the early days of 1942 they were in short supply.

For this reason, among others, it was not possible to take Len away from his radio duties as early as he wanted. He was disappointed that he was not allowed to take part in the attack on the Gorgopotamos bridge, because our Commanding Officer, Eddie Myers, needed him in the rear to report the outcome to our HQ in Cairo. (It was some comfort that the outcome was a brilliant success.) Only in 1943 was he able to take a more active role. It was a frustrating time for him at first, until we acquired more up-to-date W/T equipment. Len did not exaggerate the difficulties of communication in the early days. He also gave, in his talks with John Simpson, a vivid and accurate picture of the shortcomings of SOE in launching operations. 'From what I know now', to quote from the heading of Chapter 4, 'planning was bloody near criminal.'

'From what I know now' is the key phrase, as it probably is in the experience of all survivors from those days. It was not until 1972 , when the official embargo on secret records was cut from fifty years to thirty, that I began to learn what problems in the rear we had to try to overcome in the field. Len is inclined to blame his own officers for concealing from the Other Ranks what was really going on behind the scenes, and we were inclined to blame our superiors in Cairo for the same thing. But those were the days of 'Theirs not to reason why . . .' And it was especially important for members of SOE in the field not to know too much, in case we were captured. The Nazis had no scruples about torturing SOE prisoners, even men captured in uniform; and Hitler had condemned us to automatic execution on capture, under his 'Commando Order', which was issued in the same month (October, 1942) as our first arrival in Greece.

Len makes a fair and interesting distinction between the formality with which he was treated in the field by officers from his own country and the more easygoing attitude of our officers from New Zealand. I had noticed it myself, and when I took over command of our unit I tried to relax discipline in a similar way. I knew that this was normal form in the SAS, in which Len had served and was to serve again, and which I had been about to join myself when the Gorgopotamos operation came up instead. Some of my British officers, including a very austere Australian, disapproved of my innovation of using first names between all ranks, and I earned a reprimand from my commanding Brigadier in Cairo. But it seemed to me that the New Zealanders' attitude to discipline was about right. So, no doubt, did Len; nevertheless, the only officer who ever brought Len before me on a charge was a New Zealander!

Naturally, I can only speak at first hand of Len during the time I knew him in Greece and on Mount Carmel. In those days I learned to appreciate his quiet courage, initiative and loyalty; nor could I be unaware of the daredevil streak in his character. For the rest of his astonishing career I can only speak at second hand, but there is nothing in John Simpson's account that is incredible to me. If Len's memory is a little hazy on one or two points, there is little surprising in that: so is mine, after half a century.

Len was a restless soul, who must have found the postwar years sometimes a bit dull. He was always a boy soldier at heart. He used to ring me up from time to time: I was never quite sure from where. He finally settled in Australia, but I saw him for the last time, with John Simpson, on a visit to London. Although he was by then a retired Major, his boyish look had changed little: I should have recognized him at once, even behind his modest moustache. It was a matter of great regret that when the fiftieth anniversary of the Gorgopotamos operation was celebrated on the site in November, 1992, with survivors assembling from Greece, Great Britain, India, Israel and New Zealand, Len was the only one who could not make the journey because of failing health. But he was cheered to hear several of us talk to him in Brisbane by telephone from Athens, which was a good deal easier than talking from Greece to Egypt by radio had been half a century earlier.

He died on 24 May, 1993.

C. M. Woodhouse

ACKNOWLEDGEMENTS

In unravelling, verifying, or establishing the balance of probabilities of Len Willmott's remarkable career, I have had unstinted help from a large number and great variety of people. If, inadvertently, I have left anyone out, it is largely due to the chaos of my filing system after a move back to England from Australia, exacerbated by losing a key address book.

First and above all, my thanks to the subject himself, Len Willmott, for his quite remarkable patience, unfailing courtesy and humour, even when I resorted to something close to interrogation methods to test the truth. And I don't suppose for a minute that Len would have gone through with it without the unfailing support of the girl he proposed to when behind enemy lines in 1942 and married in 1944. If ever there was a love story, that is one.

Then the patience, encouragement and good humour of my agent Andrew Lownie who has persevered with publishers and with me. I hope one day I will reward him with a best seller.

To Monty Woodhouse (Colonel The Hon C. M. Woodhouse DSO OBE), a man who has packed more into a lifetime than half a dozen lesser mortals, I am deeply indebted for writing the charming and thoughtful Foreword.

In researching Len's boyhood and boy service, I am particularly indebted to his sister Yvonne and his brother John. The Willmotts are a remarkable family. Coming from poor and harsh beginnings, three of the four boys were commissioned during the war, two in the RAF, and had distinguished and useful postwar careers, the fourth became a grammar school headmaster, and Yvonne a director and partner in her husband's successful clothing business. Her son is one of Melbourne's premier architects.

To Michael Foot, wartime SAS officer, distinguished historian, and official historian of SOE, I am most indebted for his guidance and encouragement, and for uncovering one quite extraordinary coincidence.

To Chris Blessington (Lieutenant-Colonel C. D. A. Blessington, Royal Signals) I am indebted for a most remarkable response from the MOD. He has subsequently become a personal friend and a regular and trusted navigator on my yacht.

As I have said in the Preface, I have not always followed the advice or opinions of the two incumbents of the office of SOE Adviser during the preparation of this book, and I recognize that both will disagree with some of my conclusions. I am none the less immensely grateful to both for the enormous amount of help they have given me notwithstanding, and for some very detailed extracts from wartime SOE archives.

It is impossible to give a paragraph to everyone who has helped, or the acknowledgements would be longer than the book. I list them in alphabetical order with my sincere thanks to each and every one of them for their patience and help; even when that help was negative there was value in it:

Vera Adkins, OBE; Lt-Colonel Eric Barrass, OBE, Secretary of the Rolls Royce Enthusiasts Club; RSM Bob Bennett, MM, BEM, one of the SAS originals; Ronnie Bloom, formerly FCO; Lt-Colonel Tommy Boileau, OBE, Len's Company Commander as a Boy Soldier; Colonel Maurice Buckmaster, CBE; Brigadier Michael Calvert, DSO; Rob Chaloner, President Sydney SAS Association; Michael Clive, CB, MC, SOE and Foreign Office; Jim Collyer, formerly 1 SAS; Lt-Colonel Johnny Cooper, MBE, DCM, another original; Major John Daw, BEM, Royal Signals; Herr Eddy de Roever; Colonel A. Dewarvrin, DSO, MC (*Colonel Passy*); Colonel Sir Douglas Dodds-Parker; Major G. N. Donaldson, Royal Signals; Baron P. L. d'Aulris de Bourouill; Lt-Colonel Dennis Ewart-Evans; my cousin Angela Frater in South Africa; Lt-General Sir George Gordon-Lennox, KBE, CB, CVO, DSO, who as Major Gordon-Lennox deprived Len of his Lance Stripe in 1941; Peter Staal Gower, Jacob Staal's son; John Hall, Rolls Royce Enthusiasts Club; Major Andy Harfield, BEM, FRHistS, Curator of the Royal Signals Museum; Dr J. H. Hers Ph, Internst; Rear Admiral Richard Hill, CB, Editor of *The Naval Review*; Major Paddy Howley, MBE, Royal Signals; Former Ambassador H. C. Jorissen, DSC; Major Norman Lane, Royal Signals; Major Leo Lees, Royal Signals; Major Alastair McGregor, DSO, MC, wartime and post-war SAS; Frixos Mahas; Dr K. G. J. Margry; Leo Marks, MBE; Dr Alex Muirhead, MC, commanding an SAS Squadron one of the first men to reach Belsen; Brigadier E. C. W. Myers, CBE, DSO, commander of Op HARLING in Greece; Major Dare Newell, OBE, 'Godfather to the SAS'; Keith Richardson, ex-SAS, whose professional skills have made many of the photographs publishable; Duncan Ridler, MM, Intelligence Sergeant of 1 SAS in France and probably the first Allied soldier to enter Belsen; Major Pat Riley, CGM, DCM, one of the wartime SAS 'greats'; Major John Roper of Phantom; Ida Rose, Rolls Royce Sydney; Captain H. A. Schoofs, MBE, a Swiss-born Dutchman recruited in the Cameroons, who commanded the Signal Detachment on Op ALOES in Brittany; Reg Seekings, DCM, MM, another original and David Stirling's driver in the Western Desert; Lt-Colonel D. A. H. Sievwright, Defence Attaché in the Republic of Cameroun; Andrzej Suchcitz, MA, Assistant

Keeper of Archives, Polish Institute; Colonel Sir David Stirling, DSO, OBE; Lt-Colonel (QM) Tanky Smith, MBE; Colonel David Sutherland, CBE, MC; Mark Tadixz, whose curiosity about Len's Netherlands Bronze Lion started all this; Herr C. C. van den Heuvel; Nancy Wake, GC, OBE; Yeoman of Signals Bill Weatherall, Royal Signals; Rosamund Wilde, one of the few foreign holders of the Netherlands Resistance Cross, for some invaluable translation from the Dutch; Sir Peter Wilkinson, KCMG, DSO, OBE, without who's assessment of the Polish story I might not have gone ahead; and Lt-Colonel Pat Winter, OBE, Adjutant of 22 SAS in Malaya.

Last, and by no means least, my wife Jocelyn and my erstwhile publisher daughter Trisha for their encouragement and support.

PREFACE

Anzac Day, Sydney, 1985. As the bugle sounded 'Reveille' at the Cenotaph to greet a cloudless sunlit day, with just a hint of the southern hemisphere autumn to come, so, slowly like a flooding tide, thousand upon thousand of Australians gathered to pay homage to Australia's dead of two world wars and many lesser conflicts since. 25,000 men and women marched through Sydney that day, seventy years after the Australian and New Zealand Army Corps had won immortality at Gallipoli, and forty since the end of the Second World War.

As a 'New Australian', I marched in the parade for the first time. Next to me in the ranks of the multi-national SAS contingent was a small bespectacled man in his mid-sixties, the sort of man who is not noticed even in a small crowd. But he was wearing eleven brightly polished medals, four of them decorations for gallantry from three countries.

At the reunion that followed, a Dutchman in the contingent, having established in the shorthand common to those who have been in the secret world that both had worked for SOE, asked him where he had won his Netherlands Bronze Lion (Holland's second highest gallantry award). The reply was a modest 'Arnhem, I think, but it might have been Apeldoorn because I went in a second time.'

The Dutchman wrote off to Holland and back with the citation came the information that the authorities had been looking for a Second Lieutenant Willmott for many years, as it was the wish of the Dutch Government to award him the Netherlands Resistance Cross for his work in getting British servicemen and Dutch resistance workers out of Holland post-Arnhem.[1]

Eighteen months later, on 31 October, 1986, Major (Retired) Leonard Richard Douglas Willmott, MM, BEM, *Croix de Guerre* and Bronze Lion, was invested with his fifth decoration for gallantry by HE The Netherlands Ambassador to Australia, on behalf of HM Queen Beatrix of The Netherlands, in the presence of HE The Governor of New South Wales, a much decorated 'Pathfinder' pilot, and some 150 others. It was forty-two years and one month exactly since he had dropped, for the second time, into occupied Holland.

As a former SAS Commander, I made some enquiries through my own channels, then asked Len if I could try a book on his life. Slowly, at first reluctantly, but always modestly, he started to tell me his story.

It is an extraordinary story, the more so because Len Willmott still does not think that he did anything out of the ordinary. To my knowledge he had only spoken about his past to one other person and that in unusual circumstances shortly after coming out of Greece in 1944: Sir Horace Clive's letter to his wife is itself a quite extraordinary coincidence unearthed by Professor Michael Foot some forty-five years later.[2]

Michael Foot is the official SOE historian, and with his permission and that of HMSO, it is perhaps appropriate to quote extracts from his *SOE in France* (HMSO 1966). Referring to the official documents that faced him at the beginning of his researches, he writes:

'But only a few pebbles in this mountain pile of documentation were contributed by SOE; for unless a secret service remains secret, it cannot do its work.'[3]

He continues:

'One of the obstacles to the historian of any secret service is therefore inherent in his subject matter: the traces left for him to study are likely to be few.

'In the case of this service [SOE] there are several more. One is the problem of definition: SOE's boundaries were fluid, and it is not always easy to tell whether a particular operation was the responsibility of SOE or of some other authority, British or Allied. Again some degree of suspicion is prudent among the papers of such an ephemeral wartime organization as SOE . . . This at least can be said about the files that survive: they are in a state of authentic confusion, and are often hard to reconcile with each other; occasionally a single file is self-contradictory. Hardly any two SOE files agree, for instance, about the exact date an agent went into the field . . .

'"F", "RF", "DF", "EU/P", the "JEDBURGHS", and "EMFFI" all kept their papers in separate places classified on individual plans.'

I have had no direct access to SOE files, but two successive 'SOE Advisers' who hold what SOE records remain have been extraordinarily helpful. I will not mention their names as both are distinguished, retired, but still very much alive, and both have been members of an organization which until very recently did not officially exist. To both I am genuinely grateful and, if I have failed to follow some of their advice, it is simply because I, and others much more distinguished than I, with relatively minor reservations, believe that on the balance of probabilities, Len's accounts of his activities are accurate. See letter from Sir Peter Wilkinson to the author at Appendix 1.

However, this is Len Willmott's story which, with the help of Mark Adkin, I hope I have recorded faithfully, while doing justice to that small outwardly unremarkable and modest man, whom, over the long period of getting this story into print, I have come to admire more and more — more than ever now that he faces a terminal illness with the same quiet modesty, humour, pragmatism and courage that he faced so much else in an eventful life.

John Simpson
Sydney and Hampshire
1986–1992

Postscript

This book went to press while Len was still alive, though terminally ill, and that is reflected in the text.

On 25 May, 1993, my yacht double reefed on passage from Alderney to Lymington, I received a message via Weymouth Radio that Len had died the previous evening in Tweed Heads, New South Wales. The message is logged at 1125A and the yacht's position as 50.14′.54″N, 01.59′.31″W. No doubt the sea and conditions would have been familiar to Len in his early days as a 'Ships Tiger'.

As a courtesy to the founder of the SAS Sailing Association, my navigator on that trip, I was wearing a SAS burgee in the crosstrees. It was flown at the dip for the remainder of the voyage.

A few weeks later I saw Connie in Brisbane. She was, as I would expect, 'marvellous'. Len had died as he had lived, quietly, courageously and without fuss. He asked some other visitors to leave as he was tired, told Connie that he loved her, but wanted to 'rest now'. When Connie got home, the telephone was ringing. . . .

John Simpson
Brisbane
June, 1993

CHAPTER ONE

MAKING THE MAN

'I don't think I was ever frightened of my father; but he had a terrible temper. He had been gassed during the Great War so when he was angry, which was often, he would gasp for breath. I learned to do as I was told at once, without question. It helped my mother.'

'Right Willmott, bend over.' Boy signaller Len Willmott stood motionless for a brief moment, before hastening to comply with Company Sergeant Major 'Piggy' Johnstone's curt order. He was not unfamiliar with his predicament. Although only fifteen years old he had long ago lost count of the number of times he had had a thrashing from his father, who by an odd coincidence had also been a sergeant-major and was entitled to the same medal ribbons as Johnstone for service on the Western Front. But there was a difference. Now he was to receive an unofficial military punishment for an offence of which he was undoubtedly guilty. The six strokes of the bamboo cane were the maximum permitted. His beatings at home, which had been with belt and buckle, had gone on and on until his father had seemed on the point of collapse out of sheer exhaustion and lack of breath. Sometimes Len had thought, even wished, he was about to expire so scarlet was his face, so choking and wheezing his breathing.

As Johnstone raised his arm to strike Len clenched his jaw, involuntarily tauntened the muscles in his buttocks, as he grimly resolved not to yell out. As he was to say many years later:

'You took it, and then it was over and you got on with life. I don't think any of us had any lasting scars, physical or mental. Anyway, I'd never given my father the satisfaction of crying or begging for mercy, so I was damned if I was going to give it to the Army.'

Flogging had been abandoned as a punishment for soldiers for seventy years, but for boys in uniform in 1937 a caning was not uncommon. It was administered for serious offences which would otherwise be punishable with long periods in the cells. Boy soldiers had a choice. Len could accept the beating now or serve a sentence of detention when he came to man service at

1

eighteen. Like most of his companions he preferred to get it over with. What was the point of having a sentence hanging over you for months, if not years? Starting man service with weeks in a cell for a crime long forgotten was not a happy prospect. Neither at the time — or since — had Len ever found that caning was a punishment permitted under military law. It was common in the schools for those days, so its occurrence in boys' units within the Army would have raised no eyebrows.

Len was well aware he deserved what was coming. He had admitted to theft. He was serving in F (Boys) Company at the Royal Signals Training Brigade camp at Catterick where he had made something of a name for himself among his peers for leading raids on nearby orchards and kitchen gardens for apples or strawberries. On one of his solitary rambles he had discovered a chicken farm about three miles from barracks where, he reasoned, the absence of a few eggs or the odd hen would not be noticed. Every now and then, with two or three friends, after lights out Len would lead the way over the fence, creep up to the farm, grab a few eggs or snatch a chicken and have a barbecue on the moor. Eventually he became careless, bringing back eggs in his pockets. They broke as he clambered into camp and, despite his best efforts, his uniform remained conspicuously stained.

His Company Commander, a captain, had sentenced him to a beating, but the penalty was delayed for a week or more as his parents' permission had to be obtained first — not that Len's father was likely to object. On the appointed day Len was marched, under escort, minus belt and cap, into the Company Office. There he faced a daunting assembly of the military hierarchy. Present were the Company Commander, the Orderly Officer, the Orderly Sergeant, the Medical Officer and, of course, the Sergeant-Major. Even though his friends had told him what to expect, even though he was no stranger to pain, even though he had opted to take the beating, Len was only a young lad. He was scared.

The reasons for the presence of so much rank were prudence and prac-ticality. There was a need for strict supervision, for witnesses, so that there could be no subsequent allegations of undue brutality or buggery. The Captain directed proceedings while the Medical Officer examined the boy after each stroke. The actual beating was the duty of the Sergeant-Major with the offender bent over a table, his wrists held by the Orderly Officer and his ankles by the Orderly Sergeant. A savage, some would say sadistic, scene.

It was also a lengthy process. Len listened grimly as his Company Commander read out details of his offence, heard that his father had consented and, finally, submitted to a cursory examination by the doctor.

Next there was the business of being held down over the table. He felt totally vulnerable, helplessly exposed and ashamed, but desperately wanted it over and done with. He knew what the pain was going to be like, it was something he had to get through without tears, without breaking. He heard the familiar order, 'Carry on Sergeant-Major', felt the first flash of agony and the tightening of the grip around his wrists and ankles as his body involuntarily twisted. He heard the count of 'One.' Len sensed rather than saw the Medical Officer glance at his backside and check he had not fainted before nodding at the Sergeant-Major. Again the swish; again the pain; again the count; again the brief pause. By the fourth stroke he knew he was bleeding. His buttocks were on fire, but he refused to faint and screwed up his will not to cry out — so there was no remission. Afterwards all filed out except the doctor who ordered him to 'Drop your breeks'. Passed fit, Len walked away stiffly but dry-eyed back to his barrack room.

By fifteen Len was what we would today call street-wise. Physically he was small and thin, which soon earned him the nickname 'Titch', but he had experienced poverty, privation and pain to an extent that gave him a mental toughness, a hardness and strength of character. These attributes were not at first apparent in the undersized, scruffy lad who had to be given extra rations when he joined up. Outwardly he was an ordinary working-class youngster. Certainly none of his former officers during his boy service recall anything special about Len. His was not a face or a personality that stood out; yet, within nine years, Len Willmott, the underfed lad with little education, was a Captain with the Military Medal, British Empire Medal and *Croix de Guerre*. His wartime career in the Special Operations Executive (SOE) was perfectly suited to making an asset of his outward ordinariness, and his inward resilience of character. Len's characteristics were the product of his upbringing.

Len was born in Battersea in 1921, the son of ex-Sergeant-Major Arthur Willmott and his half-French wife Georgette. Georgette had been brought up in France, and during the First World War became a despatch rider, riding her father's horses from the family haulage business and, even under shellfire, delivering messages on the lines of communication. It was during this time that she met, fell in love with, and married against her family's wishes, a Warrant-Officer of the Royal Army Service Corps — Arthur Willmott. It was the start of a life of unremitting, grinding drudgery. Hers was the herculean task of bringing up a family of six children during the inter-war years of slump and depression, with a husband who was always brutal, frequently besotted, and often out of work.

At that time Arthur Willmott had a job as an engine driver with Southern Railways, a skill Len believes he had acquired before the First World War in India in the Royal Engineers Transportation Corps. Therein lies the mystery of the Willmott family origins. Len's second brother John writes:

'I'm afraid the truth about my father died with my mother, if she ever knew the full truth. I remember many times asking him about his background, but never getting very far. He did admit his family name was McRae, but neither he nor mother would ever explain why or when he changed his name. There was some deep secret which neither would ever reveal. . . . He did reckon to have spent a number of years in India . . . and let slip once that he had served in the Army in India. His whole background was secret including his age, as he was apparently older than he claimed.'[1]*

Len accepts that he will never know the truth about his father's origins. He despised his father for the dreadful way he treated his children and his wife. Until Willmott senior died in 1947 Len had no affection for him, merely stating that, 'He was an unusual man that I never understood'. For example he never remembers his father going to bed. He had a chair with a footrest in the living room and always seemed to sleep there. When Len started paper delivery rounds his father would wake him at 4.30 a.m. fully clothed with the fire still burning in the living room. Like most small boys, if he had a nightmare he would creep into his mother's bed — 'Father was never there'. But whatever his background it was obvious to his children that he had a good education 'just from the books he read, and he was a great letter-writer'.

Len does not recall Battersea, although his eldest sister Yvonne does.[2] She remembers her father losing his job with Southern Railways: 'It was awful, with father round the house all day, morose and angry'. He later got a job as a foreman in a limekiln in Sussex, so the family moved to Newhaven. Len, then only five, remembers this time as reasonably happy as his father went from work to the pub, and never got home before closing time. The kiln did not pay high wages and booze had first call on what was available, so Georgette also went out to work. Even so, cash was always scarce. There was an arrangement with the baker to buy yesterday's bread; it was stale and therefore a farthing a loaf cheaper. There was little money for coal so the family collected driftwood on the beach. There was no money for luxuries like jam, so much time was spent collecting blackberries and elderberries from the hedgerows, from which Mrs Willmott made jam to sell to buy sugar. There was no money for butter so they helped with milking at the farms for an occasional jug of milk. Normally they had margarine or dripping — perhaps not untypical for poor families in those days.

In 1928, with two more young children in the family, Arthur and John, Arthur senior got the sack from the limekiln. There was not enough money to pay the few shillings a week rent for the dilapidated WAC hut on the Downs that had been their home, so the family moved into a hostel. Within

* See Source Notes p. 143.

a few months Mrs Willmott took on more work, so they were able to afford a small, two-up, two-down terraced house in Newhaven. Len, now seven, remembers this as home and as the time he, too, had to start work. His meagre wages, as a paperboy, and later as a greengrocer's delivery rounds-man at weekends, made the difference between the house and the hostel. Len recounts the funny side of life:

'The greengrocer's job was a laugh. His delivery bike was one of those heavy, old-fashioned machines with a great iron basket on the front handlebars. I was so small I could only ride it underneath the crossbar, and had quite a few spills till I mastered the technique. I would have to take myself off to a quiet spot where I could clean up the vegetables that had fallen in the mud. If some of the customers only knew.'

Although Len can laugh at it now, it was a gruelling routine for a seven-year-old. Up at 4.30 he had to complete the first paper round by 7 o'clock, back for a spartan breakfast, then school by 8 o'clock, returning for tea in late afternoon, followed by the evening round. 'I didn't feel much like homework at the end of the day.' In fact his education suffered severely, to the extent that much of his early Army career was to be devoted to catching up. Every weekend he reported to the greengrocer after breakfast and kept going until all deliveries were completed.

From then on Len does not remember his father in a regular job. Mr Willmott would visit the Labour Exchange, perhaps get work for a week or so before his drinking problem resulted in another dismissal. Willmott senior had become unemployable, spending more and more time in the pub; this was 1929 with the country stricken by a slump which put millions out of work.

For the family home life was hellish, with none of the children escaping the constant rages and frequent violence. When their father returned to the house there was never a kind word for anyone. No matter how hard they had worked it was always shouting and criticism for whatever had been done or not done. Even now none of the children cares to reveal details of their suffering. As Yvonne puts it, 'I cannot talk to this day about what else went on.' At twelve she had gladly gone off to boarding school at Canterbury to escape, although who paid the fees she has no idea, unless the money came from her mother's family in France.

With Yvonne, the eldest, away Len had to bear the brunt of his father's dark moods. He was singled out for blame for the most trivial matters.

'If one of my brothers came home from school with a grazed knee or torn trousers it was my fault, and it was 'upstairs and wait for me with your trousers down'. I just learned to take my medicine and say nothing. It made it easier for Mother.'

Yet with the passage of years there was perhaps a mellowing, a touch of pride to be found in ex-Sergeant-Major Willmott. When he died Yvonne found in the old tweed jacket he wore most days two tattered, much-thumbed letters, both from Headquarters Force 133 (one of SOE Cairo's many cover names). They advised Mr Willmott of the award of the Military Medal (MM) and British Empire Medal (BEM) to his eldest son. They had the appearance of being much read and possibly much shown around the pub. Yvonne put the letters away and, as she did not see Len for another five years, forgot about them. Len had no idea they existed until late 1987. They do not, however, alter his views on his father.

One day, in the summer of 1934, Mr Willmott arrived home in an abnormally good mood, bringing with him the skipper of a Grimsby trawler which had put into Newhaven for repairs. He and the captain had known each other during the First World War. 'The next day Father took me to the docks and left me sitting on a bollard while he went on board the ship for a pint and a yarn.' Len was then thirteen and fascinated by the trawler's sturdy lines, polished brasswork and neatly coiled nets. Unable to contain his curiosity he slipped up the gangway. Within minutes he was startled by an iron grip on his shoulder. 'What are you up to, nipper? Looking for a berth?' Len whirled round to confront a small grizzled figure in a blue stripped apron, carrying a large fish-gutting knife. Without thinking he said, 'I wouldn't mind'.

Within a month Len had joined the MFV *Dove* as 'Ship's Tiger'. His excitement and delight at getting away from home were tinged with guilt at leaving his mother. The *Dove* carried a crew of eight — Bob Hunt the skipper, an engineer, three deckhands, Fred the cook — who was much the oldest — and Len as general dogsbody. It was no picnic, but he enjoyed it, and he earned good money. The *Dove*'s main fishing grounds were in Icelandic waters where some of the most savage weather in the world is to be found. Len thought the winter months the hardest, when the trawlers iced up and everyone spent hours chipping it off, even when the trawls were out. If there was a big sea it was hell, for the spray froze wherever it hit the deck, machinery or superstructure.

Whatever the weather, fishing was paramount. If they were in a good fishing patch there would be no respite. As soon as the trawls were in and the fish stowed, out they would go again. If it was a bad patch it could be extremely tedious, but Len as Ship's Tiger still had to be on deck to fetch and carry for the skipper or the deckhands. Not a minute was wasted as it meant money for the owners. There were no set hours so they took their sleep when they could. Sometimes Len would fall asleep on deck, waking up to find one of the crew had stripped off his oilskins before putting him in his bunk.

It was the way the other members of the crew looked after him that Len remembers most. They were tough hard fishermen, and their humour rough but, 'I'd never really been looked after before; Mother was just too busy, and Father, well, I think he was glad to see the back of me, and know I was earning.' The crew would watch Len, and if they saw him flagging or shivering it would be, 'Nip down to the galley, Len, and make some cocoa,' or, 'Nip below, Len, and light my pipe,' so that he could get a few moments of warmth. There were all kinds of other small kindnesses. Coming back on board after a spot of leave Fred would unexpectedly produce a bar of chocolate, or another member of the crew would produce an apple. 'I was treated as a cross between a mascot and a son by all of them.'

In heavy weather, of which they saw plenty, Len had the indignity — as he saw it initially — of having a rope tied round his waist with the other end secured to a rail on the wheelhouse. 'I had to drag this bloody thing round the deck like a ball and chain, but I soon saw the sense of it.' Trawling machinery is dangerous and, although Len helped haul in the catches, he was never allowed abaft of the winches, and there was always someone to keep a weather eye on him. If the seas were really bad, he would be sent below.

Len developed a great affection and respect for these professional fishermen, the teamwork, camaraderie and their attention to safety. One of his jobs was to look after the first-aid box, and he was forever scurrying below to get it. There were a lot of minor accidents in that sort of work, but luckily never a serious one in the *Dove* while he was there. Len learned a lot of rudimentary medicine, principally from Fred the cook, which was to stand him in very good stead in the war.

'I learned to stitch up cuts, and Fred had some unusual ideas about poultices. He'd cover an inflamed cut with rotting fruit skins to draw the pus, and it worked. He used to say that he'd discovered penicillin before Fleming.'

Typically, they were at sea for six to eight weeks at a time, followed by three to ten days in port. Bob Hunt would give Len a ticket, tell him when to be back and send him off home. His wages were five or six shillings a week, and he had something like a half of a half of a share in the catch. It was good money for a boy, and with a good catch he could take home as much as £10 to £12 after ship's deductions. 'Father's first question was always how much had I got, but I always gave the money to Mother. She would give me a bob or two back for myself when she could.'

Len was happy at sea. Small and wiry, and fit from his newspaper rounds and wrestling with the greengrocer's bicycle, he was as hard as nails at the end of a year, but, despite plenty of good food and sea air, he still did not grow much. The other aspect of trawler life which Len liked was having a place of his own which was inviolate. He had his bunk, locker and sea bag, and was completely self-contained in a tiny cubby hole for'ard of the fo'c'sle.

Len did not see a long-term future as a fisherman, and left because he wanted to join the Navy. There was to be bitter disappointment. His education was not up to it, and he failed the written entrance test. His father decided Len must have a settled career 'with prospects'. The greengrocer offered a permanent position, but to a boy of Len's spirit the prospect was awful. His father agreed to let him try for the Army. Whether he actually passed the written test, or his father knew the recruiting sergeant from the pub, or the recruiting sergeant was a perceptive man and recognized Len's quick intelligence, is uncertain — but he got through.

Accepted in September, 1935, Len had to wait until the following July, such was the competition for places in boys' regiments. Just before joining up, although he had not seen her for four years, Len made the journey to Canterbury to tell Yvonne his news. Yvonne remembers an excited Len bursting into the shop where she was working and announcing that he was joining up and would take her out to lunch. 'Oh yes, I remember that journey,' says Len. 'I'd had a pint to show I was a man, and went to sleep on the train back, missed the change at Lewes, and was woken up by the train cleaners in Brighton.' The stationmaster sent him home in a mail van, and his father gave him his last belting. 'I told him what would happen if he tried again.'

Thus Leonard Richard Douglas Willmott was recruited by Sergeant R. Thorp, medically examined by Lieutenant-Colonel T. J. White RAMC, and attested at Brighton by Major H. E. Nash, Senior Recruiting Officer Surrey and Sussex Zone, on 1 July, 1936.[3] On 2 July, as a Boy Apprentice Wireless Operator and Linesman, Len reported to 'F' (Boys) Company, Royal Corps of Signals Training Regiment, Catterick Camp, Yorkshire. He was just 15. His height was 4ft 8¼ inches, his weight 73 pounds and his chest, fully expanded, was 29 inches.

Boys in uniform were not new in the 1930s. For hundred of years lads much younger than Len have marched and fought alongside adult soldiers. Bloody battles like Blenheim in 1704 or Waterloo in 1815 saw boys of nine or ten beating the advance under fire, on drums half their own size. By 1936 boys' units were an established feature, designed to produce well-educated and well-trained tradesmen who could be expected to fill the senior NCO and warrant officer positions in the more technical Corps of the Army. These included Artillery, Engineers, Signals and Ordnance units. The infantry and cavalry also recruited boys, but only as bandboys or drummers. A high proportion of these young lads had remarkably successful careers with a substantial number reaching commissioned rank. At least one ex-Signals boy rose to be a major-general and Signal Officer-in-Chief.

It is a system that has been greatly expanded and developed in more modern times with the creation of Army Apprentice Schools for technical tradesmen and Junior Leaders Regiments for potential NCOs of all arms. Thirty-six years later Len himself was to return to a boys' unit when he was appointed the second-in-command of the Royal Signals Junior Leaders Regiment at Newton Abbot in Devon. Looking back he had no doubt that his boy service, coming on top of his hard childhood and months at sea, was the making of him. Already accustomed to hardship, quick-witted and practical, the Army was to give him a trade and an education. Because it was his success at Catterick, which he left as a highly skilled wireless operator, coupled with his inconspicuousness and strength of character that led to his selection for clandestine operations even before the formation of SOE, it is worthwhile to take a look at barrack life in those days in some detail.

Catterick Camp has always been the home of British Army signallers, and still is. It is what Warminster is for the Infantry, or Chatham for the Royal Engineers. In those days boys joined at fifteen in January or July each year. The intakes, of some 180–200 boys, would spend their first six months doing basic training, accommodated in a 'spider'. A spider was a barrack room which was in fact built like a letter H with fifteen boys sleeping in each leg, the washbasins and toilets being in the crosspiece of the H. Each leg had a bunk (separate room) for the junior boy NCO in charge of barrack-room routine. Len's comments on his first six months were, 'It was twenty-six bloody weeks on the square and laying a full kit every morning. If you weren't on the square you were being educated, and if you weren't being educated you were polishing your kit. We got two bob a week for our trouble.' Every six months the boys would move accommodation to make way for the new intake, gradually taking on more and more specialist training as wireless operators.

One of the first things Len recalls is that the Medical Officer put him on extra rations. He seemed so small — both skinny and short — that he quickly answered to the nickname 'Titch'. This was later alternated with 'Scruff', which reflected his somewhat individualistic approach to appearances and tidiness. The additional food was welcome; it included cod liver oil, milk mid-morning, four eggs a week instead of two and additional helpings at dinner if he wanted them. He certainly ate far better than ever his poor mother had been able to provide. He remained on a special diet until he reached the Army's minimum acceptable weight.

A day in the life of a boy soldier was, by design, a disciplined and full one. Reveille was at 6 a.m., followed by breakfast and a barrack-room inspection. The day's training programme started at 8 and, apart from a short NAAFI break at 11, and a hour for lunch (all meals were parades to which the boys were marched as a formed body), training went on until 5 p.m. Tea, the last main meal of the day, was at 5.30, except for a cup of soup and a slice of plain bread at 8 from the cookhouse.

Then there were the inevitable fatigues, barrack-room cleaning and preparation of their kit for the next day. Lights Out was at 9.30 p.m. There was a small Boys Canteen where char and wads could be purchased for a penny or tuppence, a games room with a dartboard, packs of cards and a few board games like Monopoly, plus a Quiet Room where there were newspapers and magazines and boys could write letters. Weekly letters home were mandatory and had to be produced on muster parade on Mondays.

Saturday always included a full scale barrack-room and kit inspection followed by a drill parade. After lunch there was organized sport. Sunday afternoon was really the only part of the week when a boy had some time to himself, and Len took to going for long, usually solitary, rambles on the moors.

The Boys' Company was something of a closed society, in a way not unlike an order of monks, although the boys' attitude to the other sex was anything but monastic. Discussions were literal and crude, even if based more on imagination than practical experience.

In terms of social contact, their horizons were bounded by the barrack-room, cookhouse and canteen. There was little or no contact with the civilian world. Their weekly pay was miserly: two shillings a week on joining, three when they passed the intermediate Group E tests at 16, and the princely sum of four shillings at 17, provided they had obtained their Grade III tradesman qualifications and the requisite Army Certificates of Education. Out of it the boys had to buy their own cleaning materials and meet the Army's inevitable stoppages for breakages or 'barrack damages'. Len had an additional demand on his slender purse; he had started smoking at sea and — partly because it was against the rules — he continued at Catterick, so had to find the tuppence for the occasional packet of five Woodbines. He still smokes like a chimney.

There was little left for outside entertainment apart from occasional visits to the cinema; the garrison cinema was a three-mile walk and the cheapest seats were sixpence. On a boy's pay they could manage that about once a month.

Some 20–25 percent of boys' training was straightforward education, but with some military bias to fit them for the various Army Certificates of Education. ACE 1st Class was roughly equivalent to the then School Certificate or today's GCSE. Furthermore, qualifications in military trades were tied to appropriate ACEs, so there was a strong incentive to 'pay attention and get them behind you'.

Len was very conscious of his own lack of formal education compared to most others; his jobs to help make ends meet at home from the age of 7, and going to sea at 13 had taken its toll. He was quick to realize the advantages and, though he found it a battle to start with, he was a fast learner and had his ACE 1st Class by the time he came on to man's service.

Organized sport plays an important part in any military curriculum, particularly so in boys' units. Len did not shine at sport as he did not enjoy team games. He did not share the enthusiasm of the other boys for soccer, and saw little point in kicking a ball from one end of a field to the other. Unless there were medical reasons to except them, all boys had to box, and he might have shone at boxing. Sergeant 'Shiter' Hawke, a champion middleweight himself, told Len he could be Army featherweight champion if he put his mind to it.

A contemporary boy soldier, Bill Weatherley, describes how Len got into a scrap with an older and much bigger boy in defence of another 'Titch'.

'The CSM broke it up and made them fight it out in the gym. Len went at the other bloke like a tornado and nearly killed him. No Queensberry rules and he had to be pulled off him.'[4]

Len, however, could only fight if he hated the other's guts. 'I saw no point in getting stuck into a bloke who had done me no harm.'

Len is frank about his boy service. 'I never got a stripe as a boy, and I don't think I deserved one. I was always a bit of a rebel — nothing serious, just bucking the system to see what I could get away with.' This putting one over the Army game had started in the recruiting office. When the recruiting sergeant was filling up his attestation form one inevitable question had been, 'What Religion?' Len told him that he did not go to church. 'You've got to have a religion in the Army, lad,' said the sergeant. 'If you're C of E you get marched to church every Sunday. If you're a left footer like me, you get fell out as heathen on church parade, so we'll put you down as RC.' So Roman Catholic Len has been ever since.

It suited Len at Catterick. The 'heathen' were paraded at 6.30 a.m. and despatched to walk to the garrison RC church services. As soon as they were out of sight at the bottom of the hill they would nip into a disused gym and lark about until it was time to walk back for breakfast. When they got back at about 8 or quarter-past, all the C of E boys were on parade. It meant also 'a bloody good breakfast because we could have everything that was left over'.

There was one character, an old sweat soldier who had joined up long before the First World War, whom Len always remembers with admiration and who, seemingly, encouraged him in his very earliest clandestine activities. This was Lance Corporal Tommy Blades, a man who achieved the remarkable distinction of eventually receiving a bar to his long Service and Good Conduct Medal — 'Thirty-six years of undiscovered crime' — and serving in both world wars.[5] He died in 1985 aged 96. He was clearly one of those military characters who become a legend in their own small world, usually tucked away as storemen, but wielding great influence in their sphere.

Len believes that 'Tommy had been in the Army so long that he was on some pay and ration scale that dated from the Crimean War. He ate in the cookhouse when it suited him because the cook sergeant didn't dare kick him out, but he drew ration money on top of it. The sergeants kept him in beer, otherwise they couldn't get the kit they wanted from his stores. He lived like a minor king in a bunk off the stores, and had a woman down in Catterick that he visited once a week. . . . He was very good to the boys — no nonsense mind you — but when any of the boys were on jankers [punishment] and had to be at the guardroom in full kit five minutes before reveille, Tommy Blades would come round and make certain they were up.'

Tommy was something of a minor folk hero to the boys for another reason. He had been gassed in the First World War and had lost a lung, but he regularly won the Northern Command Cross Country Championship, the last time when he was forty.

The only parade that Len remembers Tommy being on was what the Army calls a 'Scale X' parade (virtually everybody who can stand) for an inspection by HRH The Princess Royal, Colonel-in-Chief of The Royal Corps of Signals. The entire training brigade was formed up, commanded by Brigadier Jeffreys from a horse. When the Princess's car was sighted the Brigadier bellowed, 'Parade SHUN', and spat his false teeth straight over his horse's head. Len remembers vividly what happened,

'Next thing we saw was Tommy Blades marching out, cool as a cucumber. He picked them up, dusted them off, saluted, and handed them back. Next day Tommy was marched in front of the Brigadier and was excused three guards for initiative — not that he ever did guard duty — so that gave us a laugh too.'

Len became one of the privileged few with more or less unrestricted access to Tommy's bunk and stores, his illegal kettle and unofficial source of

1. (*Left*) Len as a boy soldier, Catterick Camp, 1936. (see p.8)

2. (*Below left*) "Working there was a girl called Connie. I rather liked the look of her" (p.33).

3. (*Below right*) Acting Sergeant Willmott, Cairo, 1942 (see p.37).

4. "Operation HARLING was a fundamental cock-up from the start"
(p.48). Standing, right, Tom Barnes, fourth from right, Eddie Myers,
sixth from right, Monty Woodhouse. Kneeling, left, Len Willmott.

5. Len *(right)* with a colleague, Greece, 1944.

rations. He would listen with awe to Tommy's stories of the trenches in the First World War, his off-duty exploits in pub or brothel, and his outrageous pronouncements on the Army in general or the Royal Corps in particular.

Before embarking on the farmyard raids that cost Len his caning he had put in plenty of practice on the coalyard which was located inside the barrack walls. The two back-to-back fireplaces in the barrack rooms were hopelessly inadequate for heating in winter and consumed enormous quantities of coal, which was strictly rationed. Len's room, however, was seldom short. 'I used to organize raids over the barbed wire of the coal yard. Tommy Blades had some sort of responsibility for it, amongst many other things, so I always knew when to go in.' One of the Sergeant Instructors, Sergeant Barlow (known out of earshot as Barlow the Bastard) had a shrewd suspicion that Len was the ringleader but could never catch him. As a somewhat backhanded compliment he told Len that he would make 'boy sergeant' if he put as much effort into soldiering as he put into getting into trouble.

This was a little harsh. Len was indeed working hard. The regime was demanding, as Bill Weatherley remembers, 'It was morse, morse, and more morse. Morse on key, morse with lamps, morse with flags, morse with helio, until you lived, breathed, ate and dreamed morse.'[6] There were two Sergeant Instructors. One nicknamed, somewhat unkindly, 'Kipper' (which was supposed to indicate his being two-faced and having no guts), and Barlow. Barlow's unorthodox methods of teaching are still recalled. He literally drummed morse into the boys heads. 'If anyone missed a letter Barlow would come round behind him and clap his bloody great hands over their ears to the rhythm of the morse. By the end of a lesson many ears would be red and stinging — but we learned fast.'

In spite of Len's somewhat ambivalent attitude to authority, and not infrequent brushes with it, when it came to wireless operating he was the pure professional. To him, receiving well-transmitted high-speed morse was pure music, and getting the right rhythm on the key when transmitting himself gave him the sort of satisfaction he thinks accomplished pianists must get.

A Captain Coles in the technical wing came up with the idea of the boys building a transmitter. It was a largely private enterprise affair as Coles had family connections with a major electronics firm who provided many of the parts free. It took them a year and Len was one of the boys who put in a lot of extra hours. He was not a wireless mechanic, but he was always happy to help. It was to stand him in good stead in the war.

'I had an advantage on most SOE wireless operators because I knew the basics of how sets worked and could very often sort out technical problems without the help of a mechanic — anyway there were precious few wireless mechanics where I served.'

When the transmitter was finished the War Office, impressed with the quality of signals with Singapore, decided to make the 'boys' transmitter' the principal link to the Far East. It was quite an achievement in 1937. Len loved it and was always ready for extra duty on the set.

'You would tap out your callsign, and it was always magic to me to hear the answering call from the other side of the world, and the adrenalin runs as you fine tune to hold him.'

By the time he left Catterick, Len was proud of the fact that he could take morse at thirty words a minute, from the fastest of the operators at the other end in Singapore: 'You are reading three or four sentences, sentences not words, behind what you are writing, but it becomes another language.' He learned, also, from the Far East link, many of the operator's tricks of the trade. All morse operators have a 'signature' which other professionals quickly recognize. There are other, unofficial ways, that operators managed to pass personal messages — something Len was to use to advantage later.

Len made few close friends at Catterick, none who survived the war. Comrades who knew him say that he was both popular and respected by the other boys. By his final year, without the formal authority of a 'stripe', he had emerged as someone to whom even the boy NCOs listened. It was then 1938 and Len was seventeen. He was looking forward eagerly to coming on to man service in the following July, but was totally unaware, and would never have believed it if told, that he had already been talent-spotted for special training — precisely by whom we are never likely to know. Officially, MI6 does not exist.

CHAPTER TWO

A FUNNY WAY TO GO TO WAR

'Wedged between a large woman and the window my head gradually fell forward on to her ample bosom. It was more comfortable than the window. It was also a funny way to go to war.'

Signalman Len Willmott was almost certainly the only British soldier to have been on the River Oder in Germany, the virtual startline for much of the German attack on Poland, at H-hour on 1 September, 1939. Not that he had the remotest inkling of what was happening or why he was there, struggling to reach Warsaw, the capital city of the first country to experience the impact of a blitzkreig assault. The Second World War was then within minutes of starting.

At dawn on that day Len was in Breslau, a German town on what was then the Polish border, directly in the path of General Blaskowitz's eight infantry divisions who had been ordered to advance to contain the Polish Army centred on the city of Lodz. To the north and south armoured formations were poised to form pincers designed to outflank the Polish defences, cut off her armies and surround Warsaw, thus bringing about her defeat and occupation. In the event it was to take them a mere twenty days to liquidate the Polish armed forces; within four weeks Warsaw had surrendered. The Polish losses were immense; over 100,000 were killed, 500,000 taken prisoner. Len was to remain in occupied Poland for almost eight months; thus he was in action against Hitler, albeit in a clandestine role, months before any other British personnel.

Of all his wartime exploits Len's time in occupied Europe from September, 1939, through to his arrival back in England in July, 1940, was the most unprecedented. Incredibly a young lad of eighteen was (unknowingly to him) recruited, one can only assume, by the SIS; spent almost eight months with the Polish resistance; travelled over 4,300 miles through six countries, four of which were under German control; read about the German invasion of Belgium in a German newspaper in Berlin; rode on a German train under the care of a uniformed SS officer; then successfully escaped via France, Spain and Gibraltar. To this day the Foreign and Commonwealth Office refuse to acknowledge that such things could ever happen.

In March, 1938, with Hitler's annexation of Austria, Britain took the first tentative steps towards examining the possibility of clandestine warfare in Europe. SOE was still over two years away, and Britain's efforts were tiny, ill-co-ordinated and overlapping. Three bodies were set up, two under the Foreign Office and one under the War Office.[1] The first was a small internal department whose task was to look into the possibilities of propaganda, nicknamed 'EH' after its home in Electra House near the Thames. The second, also under the Foreign Office, was really part of the SIS called MI6-D (for destruction), briefed to explore how an enemy might be attacked by any means other than conventional military ones. The third was a small internal branch of the War Office, soon designated MI-R (for research), whose remit was also the much neglected subject of guerrilla operations. It was these three minor departments that Churchill, in July, 1940, was to officially combine as SOE and instruct to 'set Europe ablaze'.[2] He had then formally created the fourth branch of Britain's Armed Services. It was to exist for six years.

Within MI6-D it soon became apparent that the glue that held together any major subversive or partisan campaign would be wireless communications. Nothing much could be achieved without reliable sets and operators; no plans could be implemented, no supplies dropped, no agents moved unless secure communications were functioning behind enemy lines. It also came as a shock to discover that until then the SIS had been unable even to afford wireless sets for many of its agents.[3] Major (later Sir) Richard Gambier-Parry, Royal Welsh Fusiliers, was loaned to the SIS to head a Section VIII (communications). His primary mission was to find both the operators and sets for deployment to selected SIS stations overseas. He looked to the Merchant Navy and, to a lesser extent, the Army.

All this was totally unknown to Len, as it was to all but a handful of people in Britain. In the summer of 1938, just as he turned seventeen, possibly some innocuous official visitor to Catterick spotted Len as being a potential recruit. Probably it was his inconspicuousness, his ordinariness, coupled with his undoubted ability with a morse key, that caught the visitor's eye.

In September, 1938, Len's intake of F (Boys) Company of the Training Regiment Royal Signals had just qualified as Wireless Operators Grade 3. It meant an extra sixpence a day for each of them. They were shortly to be attached to the Liverpool GPO as telegraphists to speed up their morse. On his return Len was scheduled for a driver/operator course. Then, one morning his contentment was shattered by the arrival of his Troop sergeant, Sergeant Hawke, inevitably referred to behind his back as 'Shiter'. 'Willmott, Company Office — pronto.' As Len relates:

'Company Office usually meant trouble for the likes of me and my heart sank to my boots. But as I plodded across the square I couldn't for the life of me think what I'd done wrong recently. We had just got this new company commander with a funny French name, Boileau, who we hadn't got the measure of. He was a tall, very serious bloke — a bit like a prissy schoolmaster. He just said straight off, "You're to report to the War Office for an interview. See the Sergeant-Major for details". I started to ask about Liverpool but Boileau just snapped, "That's all." My world was shattered.'

The next day, with a letter and three shillings and sixpence ration money for three days in his pocket, Len was on a train to London.

'I'm a Londoner, Battersea born, but Whitehall was a bit out of my class. I felt a bit of a charlie in my serge service dress and boots with all these pinstripe blokes with bowlers and rolled umbrellas. A copper pointed out the War Office and I marched up the steps to an enormous bloke in a blue frock-coat with crowns on the lapels and a handlebar moustache, saluted and handed him my letter. He looked at me like I'd come out from under a stone and said, "This hentrance is reserved for members of the Harmy Council, and I hain't been advised of your appointment to it."

He wasn't a bad bloke really and told me where to go round the side where I handed over my letter to another bloke with crowns on the lapels but a less fancy coat. After a bit an officer in uniform arrived and told me to follow him. We went up several flights of stairs, along endless corridors to a bare room with a couple of tables and a few chairs. A nice old biddy gave me a cuppa and a biscuit. Then, over the next two hours, seven or eight people came in, some officers in uniform and others in civvies, and asked me a lot of questions. I hadn't a clue what they were on about, but a lot of it was straightforward — about my training and the like, what kind of frequencies I'd use by day and night, what sort of aerials (they weren't called antenna then). Some of the questions about my family I didn't like much, and one question one of the civvie types asked me I thought really odd. He wanted to know if I was sent to Gibraltar could I build my own wireless transmitter, and could it reach England.

I thought it a pretty silly question as he must have known that I was an operator not a wireless mechanic, but I told him I'd worked on the transmitter built by the boys at Catterick in their spare time, and now being used for regular traffic between the War Office and Singapore.

Then they thanked me for coming — the first time I'd been thanked for anything in the Army — and I caught a train back to Catterick.'

It had been a bewildering business. With no notice, with no reason given, without having applied for any course, Len was rushed to the War Office. As a boy soldier his experience of the military hierarchy was confined to his instructors, of whom he saw a great deal, his Sergeant-Major and Company Commander who he saw as infrequently as possible, his Commanding Officer only on rare occasions when in deep trouble or glimpsed on a formal parade — but the War Office! It was responsible for the entire Army; it was above the clouds; it was God. On the journey back Len wrestled with the extraordinary events. What was the purpose of all the queries, what possible reason could there be for asking so many questions, most of which could have been obtained by consulting his records or his Company Commander? And why such an interest in his family? He had found it difficult to describe his father. The only logical explanation he could come up with was that he was going to be posted to a War Office signals unit when he came on man service. There was no way he wanted that. But in those far-off days nobody questioned the mysterious ways of the military, least of all seventeen-year-old boys.

So Len did not go to Liverpool with his pals; instead he killed time on fatigues for nearly three weeks before a second summons arrived. This time he went in civilian clothes.

'The same officer met me but this time he took me to another building not far away, down a little lane. There were two officers in civilian clothes, one a good deal older than the other who didn't say much. The questions were pretty sharp this time, till the older bloke suddenly asked if I could drive. That put me on the spot as I'd had a few unofficial lessons from a mate in the MT to make sure I passed the driver/operator course, so I said "a little", but I wouldn't mind learning. The old bloke laughed, and I suddenly realized they knew more about me than I realized. This was to happen many times over the next few years, this sudden feeling "they know about me".'

On this occasion the questions were more discerning. How would he operate his set in varying locations or conditions — in towns, in mountains, in open country? How would he conceal his aerial? What would be the effect of rain, of heat or intense cold, on transmissions?

One can only assume that Len's interviewers had decided immediately that he was suitable for further training, and that he had been picked as a potential wireless operator for the SIS for deployment into Europe at some future date. It would all begin in earnest some nine months later when Len was sent to Poland, still entirely ignorant of the fact that he was working for the Secret Service. A remarkable recruitment system.

The training in store for Len, to prepare him for what would become highly important strategic as well as extremely hazardous missions, consisted of a comprehensive driving course, which he enjoyed enormously, and a short and terrifying course in parachuting, which he did not.

Len did not return to Catterick after his second interview. Instead he was put in a car and driven to Scotland Yard. After a police canteen meal he was driven to Cricklewood and delivered to the semi-detached home of Mr and Mrs Edwards in Evelyn Road. He had arrived at what would today be called a 'safe house' not far from the Hendon Police Driving School. The Edwards were probably retired; perhaps Mr Edwards had been a driver or porter, his wife a former typist. In this instance they provided Len with his base for his six-week driving course, and it was from Mr Edwards that Len received his routine instructions and travel money.

'The Edwards were a nice homely couple, retired I guessed, but they didn't seem surprised to see me. Mr Edwards told me a car would pick me up in the morning. A car! For me! A small insignificant 17-year-old. But you've got to realize that I came from a generation and a background that just didn't ask questions. . . . As a young lad it was fabulous, so why ask anyway? The first week I spent driving a Morris 8 round and round their [Hendon Police Driving School] ruddy great square with all sorts of obstacles on it. To begin with I had an instructor with me, then more and more I was on my own. The second week I was given a provisional licence and taken out on the roads, now always with an instructor. . . .

The third week Mr Edwards took me to the bus depot at Chiswick, but now I had to go by tube. I drew only 2/6 a week as the rest of my pay went to help my mother, but now I got a pound a week in cash for travel and food, so I used to get up early and walk most of the way. My time with the bus company was much the same as with the police, but single deckers only, and their skid pan was bloody marvellous. . . . The final two weeks were at Pickfords' Depot in Hounslow driving their vans and trucks. That was a laugh because even in the smaller vans I needed two cushions under my backside to reach the pedals, and I had to stand up to change gear. Some of the vans had seven forward and five reverse gears, so I got a lot of exercise.'

Just before Christmas, 1938, Mr Edwards gave him his pay, travel warrant, advised him not to speak of his training and sent him home on leave. Before the end of the month an official envelope was delivered. In it were yet more exciting but extraordinary instructions. Len was to report back to the War Office on 3 January in civilian clothes bringing a spare shirt and two changes of underwear — he was off to France. It seemed so preposterous that the War Office should be sending him on a trip overseas and concerning itself with his underwear. At his father's insistence they went into Newhaven to buy a new pair of trousers (Len paid), while his mother gave him an embarrassing talk on 'not getting into trouble with the girls'.

This time he was met by a major in the Royal Welsh Fusiliers, whom Len thought he recognized as having been at his first interview in civilian clothes. He told Len that he had done well so far and that he was now going to Paris to learn to drive on the right-hand-side of the road. Still he did not put two and two together — his speciality as a wireless operator, these strange summons to the War Office, never wearing uniform, the need to be able to handle all types of vehicles, and now learning to drive in France. Still he was told nothing as to where all this was leading.

'You can imagine my wonderment. I'd been to sea, but never abroad, and my mother was half French so I had a few French words — but very few. Anyway, I got to Paris Gare du something, and found a phone box. It was a bloody awful machine — you put your money in and wound a handle — and when I got through the operator didn't understand me, and I didn't understand her. Eventually I found a porter who spoke some English and he got me through, and was I pleased to hear an English voice speaking! About forty minutes later a car arrived with an officer in plain clothes — he was the assistant military attaché, I discovered later. He drove me to a house, but I couldn't tell you where. All I remember is that there was an English-woman, called Maude, about thirty-five I would judge now, old to me then, and two other Frenchwomen.

Next morning the Englishman who had met me came round. On the way we stopped off at a very impressive building which was the British Embassy, then on to a garage in back street. I was handed over to a Frenchman called Jacques, to me a typical Frenchman — moustache and black beret. But he was a wonderful driver. He took me out in all sorts of cars from the garage. A couple of times he took me into the country with his wife on a picnic. . . . I reckon that was when I developed a taste for wine.'

By the end of January he was back at Catterick. He had had strict orders to travel to Dover in plain clothes, then don uniform for the remainder of the journey. His driving licence and medical certificate, in sealed envelopes, he handed in to Sergeant-Major Johnstone, who clearly did not believe he had been sick at home all this time with gastro-enteritis as the medical certificate claimed.

It was March before he was once more summoned to London. Not unnaturally, curiosity was his dominant feeling as he was ushered in to see the Royal Welsh Fusilier major again. He was in for a shock. After a few friendly enquiries about Paris the major announced casually, 'Oh, by the way, you are off on a parachute course tomorrow.' There seemed no option. Len had not been asked to volunteer; the major seemed to speak as though it was as inconsequential as going for a stroll. At seventeen Len still held officers, particularly those sitting in the War Office, in great awe and was still too tongue-tied to voice his uncertainties. As he headed for Reading airfield worries about leaping out of aircraft prevented his seeing that this course was surely the ultimate test on the way to something special, something altogether different from run-of-the-mill signalling.

Len was right to be apprehensive. The course consisted of eight jumps and in 1939 parachuting was anything but sophisticated; some would say anything but safe. There was no static line, no reserve chute or uncompli-cated leap from a door in an aircraft's side. Instead he found, along with nine other trainees, that after some rudimentary ground instruction, he was expected to crawl out along the lower wing of an ancient bi-plane (Len's term for it was 'a right old string bag') desperately clinging to the struts as the wind tore at his body.[4] Another terrified trainee was on the other wing. When the pilot waved they were supposed to let go. After that it was up to them to pull the ripcord on their chests. Then, with luck, the blissful slow descent. It was the first time in his young life that he had to conquer real fear, to overcome the all-powerful instinct of self-preservation. That he did so was to his great credit, although Len attributes some of it to the fact that

'I was usually paired with an officer called Templer as we were the nearest in weight [to balance the wings]. His language made even me blush. The first time my innards turned to water, and Templer said, "Don't you fucking hesitate boy, or you'll be going up to the fucking angels, not down on a fucking parachute." The next time I met Templer was in 1953 in Malaya when he was a full general and High Com-missioner and I was an SAS major. His first words were, "Good God, the fucking boy signaller. Why aren't you dead?"'

On 23 June, 1939, Len finally became a man in the eyes of the Army. He almost forgot about the strange life of the past months when he received an official posting to a field unit, the 3rd Division Signals Regiment at Bulford.[5] He reported in on 5 July, only to be told on interview by his new commanding officer that should the unit go to war he would be left behind until he was nineteen. Within a month, however, his depression was dispersed by yet another call to London.

This time he sensed some sort of mission was in store. He was measured for civilian clothes by a master tailor, he was photographed, signed a passport application, and told to hand in all his uniform except for his underwear: 'That was civvie anyway as I kept the Army ones for kit inspections.' Then, accompanied by a captain, he travelled by train to Crieff in Perthshire, finally arriving after a tiring and boring journey at a large house just out of the town. It was to be known to the locals after the war as 'the auld Spook House'.[6] Len did not know it had been taken over by the SIS for courses, although he did by now realize that the unit or organization he was in was a secret one, but he assumed it was a part of the War Office signals set-up. His description of what happened there is brief and to the point:

'It was a civilian house on the outskirts of Crieff, but was full of signallers, a good many from the Merchant Navy, and they were really good. . . . I was only there about three or four days, but it was interesting and I was shown a lot of kit [wireless equipment] that I'd never seen before.'

Back in London events moved fast. His new civilian clothes arrived, he was paid in a variety of foreign currencies, briefed (as far as his journey was concerned, not about a specific mission), handed tickets to Harwich and the Hook of Holland, his passport and a sealed envelope with instructions not to open it until he reached the Hook. Finally, he was given a wireless set in three haversacks and driven to Liverpool Street station.

Signalman Willmott, although he did not know it, was off to war.

At about the time Len was hurling himself off the wings of a bi-plane, a Major Colin Gubbins from MI-R was touring Eastern Europe assessing the possibilities of partisan warfare, making contacts and tentative plans of how, in the event of war in Europe, clandestine operations could be encouraged. He visited the Baltic States — and Poland.[7] He was impressed by the Poles' potential for resistance; indeed, he was to return to Warsaw just prior to the outbreak of war as Chief-of-Staff to the British Military Mission at the British Embassy, so as to be well placed to co-ordinate British activities in this field for MI-R. Despite the Munich agreement of the previous autumn which had witnessed the British Prime Minister Neville Chamberlain waving his useless piece of paper, much of the world saw war as inevitable.[8] Italy and Japan were aligned with Germany, Austria had been absorbed, Abyssinia conquered, Czechoslovakia dismantled and Albania invaded. Poland was surely next.

At some time after Gubbins' return to London somebody in the SIS made the decision to send Len into Europe with a wireless set. From his initial travel instructions it would seem he was to be sent to Germany but, as events will show, these were soon changed to Poland. It is impossible to know exactly what his mission was as Len was never told, and to this day official sources deny he ever went. But the circumstantial evidence and the assessments of Sir Peter Wilkinson and Professor M. R. D. Foot must call that into question.

Len's channel crossing in mid-August, 1939, was uneventful, except that he had to produce his passport to prove his age before being allowed to buy a beer. It was then that he noticed he was described in it as a student. He felt somewhat peeved, so decided to open his sealed envelope. In it were several surprises. His written instructions were under a travel agent's letterhead entitled 'Tourist Itinerary'. He was to make for Munich, via Utrecht, where he would be met at the station. He was told that on no account should he keep the three wireless haversacks with him on the train. They must always be deposited in the guard's van. The necessary rail tickets were provided along with train timings.

The only incident Len recalls clearly on the journey to Munich was at the Dutch-German border where frontier police turned over everybody's baggage. He was thankful his incriminating haversacks were not with him. 'They were arrogant bastards, and put the likes of Sergeant-Major 'Piggy' Johnstone to shade. There was one poor old Frau who had her shopping kicked about the compartment with jackboots. However, I had enough sense to keep my mouth shut.'

At the platform barrier at Munich a middle-aged man greeted him with 'Welcome, Herr Willmott; I will take you to your hotel.' Exactly the words he had been told to expect. The 'travel agent' drove him for about an hour and a half by car to a small spa town some forty miles south of Munich. After nearly fifty years Len remembers the name as something like 'Otting' or 'Outing'. The small spa town of Otterfing is about 60 km from Munich. At the hotel he was handed over to the proprietor, another English-speaking German, to whom Len duly gave his wireless set as per his instructions. The hotelier took him to the cellar, opened a heavy door, put the three haversacks inside and relocked it. Nothing was said.

For the next ten days or so Len just hung around, going for walks (he avoided the town) and wondering what would happen next. He was surprised that nobody wanted him to set up his wireless. He thinks it was early on 30 August that the proprietor dashed into his room and told him to pack at once. Len was incredulous to hear that he must take his wireless to the British Embassy in Warsaw. His knowledge of Eastern European geography was pretty shaky; all he knew was that Warsaw was in Poland which was a long way from Munich. He was right; he faced a journey of some 500 miles, which included crossing Czechoslovakia.

'The man was like a cat on hot bricks until I was packed and ready to leave. He gave me a typewritten list of instructions, some German and Polish money, got the haversacks out of the cellar and drove me to Munich station where he bought my tickets. For the first time I began to feel bloody lonely.'

He changed trains at Pilsen (the German version of Plzen) *en route* to the Czech capital of Prague, since the previous year a part of Hitler's Reich. There he had to contend with a long wait for the night express to Warsaw, which was unnerving among so many German troops. He counted himself lucky that he had no difficult encounters with officialdom. At last he climbed aboard, grateful that a couchette had been reserved for him.

He woke as the train clanked to a halt in a station with a great hiss of escaping steam. It was a very final sound. He sat up to look at his watch. He was proud of his watch. He had bought it with his first pay when he had come on to man service two months earlier, and he had agonized over paying an extra half-crown to have a luminous dial. Now he was glad. In the dim light of the compartment it glowed just after 11 pm. The date — 1 September, 1939.

The conductor came through the compartment shouting something in Polish. Len stopped him to ask what he had said. 'Germany invade Poland, this train go no further,' was the reply in passable English. Len looked out of the window. It was a major station. The scene on the platform was bedlam; men and women rushing in all directions, some dragging protesting children, all loaded with baggage of every conceivable sort. The noise was deafening. Suddenly all the lights went out; then the air-raid sirens began their banshee wail.

Len had heard air-raid sirens being tested before he left England. This, he reasoned, must be for real. His reactions were disciplined and automatic. His orders had been to put the wireless haversacks in the guard's van. He part barged, part burrowed his way through the near-hysterical crowd to get to the wireless haversacks.

Panting, lugging his suitcase and the haversacks as fast as his small wiry frame allowed, he found an unoccupied corner and subsided into it. He did not know where he was, except that he was somewhere between Prague and Warsaw; he did not understand the language, nor could he decipher the name of the station — from the announcements it sounded something like 'Breezeland'. In moments of crisis, if there was nothing else to do, he did what he had always done; he went to sleep.

Len was at Breslau. He was on the Germans' start-line for their assault on Poland which had just begun, preceded by an intense aerial bombardment. The frantic crowds on the station were mostly Poles wanting to get home before the war caught up with them. For the great majority it was too late.

It was a dozing, disturbed sort of sleep with people tripping over him and, in the background, the crash of bombs exploding. By dawn he was cold, cramped and very frightened. It was a dreadful day, panic all around him, with crowds trying desperately to get on any trains that were still running. It was the only time during his months in Poland that he could not find a Pole who spoke at least a smattering of English.

The second night was worse, with hunger added to fear and bewilderment. He had Polish money, plenty of it, though he did not understand the denominations, but the food kiosks were closed.

In the cold light of the second dawn he battled his way to the ticket office again, where at last he found a clerk who spoke some English. Yes, there was a train to Warsaw but it was a stopping train. No, he did not know when it would depart; no, he did not know when it would arrive. These were difficult times.

Using the suitcase as a battering-ram, lugging 'the bloody haversacks' (by that time everything was 'bloody', particularly the haversacks), Len eventually fought his way on to the train. There was standing-room only and not much of that. Finally, after what seemed an interminable wait, the train puffed slowly out of the station. Wedged between a large woman and the window, his head gradually fell forward on to her ample bosom. It was more comfortable than the window. In Len's words, 'It was a funny way to go to war.' Back in Britain war had indeed been declared on Hitler; Signalman Willmott was behind enemy lines. The large woman whose bosom he was using as a pillow raised no objections; she actually gave him some bread and cheese from her basket. He was ravenously hungry by then, so the simple food revived his spirits. He began to take an interest in the countryside as the train 'stopped at every second lamp post like a dog'. At every stop the pantomime of people with bundles shoving and pushing to get off or on was re-enacted. At the time he thought it was quite funny. After many hours the train stopped at a station where the pandemonium was even more pronounced. Everyone was getting off.

An English-speaking railway official told him that Warsaw had been bombed, so the driver and guard had gone home. The town sounded something like 'Lewes'. He had arrived at the Polish town of Lowicz, which he was told was about eighty kilometres from Warsaw. It did not seem an impossible distance to Len, who was still intent on following his instructions. The logical way was to follow the line of the railway and, equally logically, he reasoned that he would not be able to carry the three wireless haversacks that far.

'I was pretty tired and pissed off by then, so I decided to cache the wireless where it could be recovered later.' After following the track for a mile or so he found a suitable culvert, where he stashed the haversacks inside at the rear of a dark shelf in the wall. After burning his written instructions, he found his way on to what appeared to be a main road. Apart from short lifts on a farm cart and a motorcycle, Len walked to Warsaw, unaware that he was just keeping ahead of the advancing Germans. He got food from isolated farms, occasionally buying some in villages. When really hungry he dug up potatoes or swedes from the fields and ate them raw. As he approached the city he followed the railway tracks into the marshalling yards. He had lost track of time, but estimated the date to be between 8 and 10 September. The thought that kept him going was the beckoning sanctuary of the British Embassy. Once within its gates he would be safe — almost home, even.

He sought and obtained directions from a railway worker and at last reached his goal in the centre of the city. It is not difficult to imagine his feelings, after a journey totalling almost a thousand miles by boat, train, car, cart, motorcycle and finally on his feet when he found the Embassy gates locked and the building seemingly abandoned. It was around 6 p.m. so just possibly they had shut for the night. Although he could hardly bring himself to believe this to be the case, he resolved to try again the following morning.

Second only to Breslau, the first night in Warsaw was the worst of his journey. The stimulus of making for a destination had evaporated. Finding the Embassy empty was a bitter blow. Weary, dispirited, lonely and frightened, he wandered off down a side road and found a doorway in a bombed building before slumping down wrapped in his coat. It seemed barely credible that a few short weeks ago he had been secure in his Signal Regiment at Bulford; now he was utterly alone the other side of Europe in a country whose language he could not understand, in a city under attack from the Germans. He had no contacts, no orders as to what to do, no source of food or shelter. It was with thoughts such as these in his mind that he finally dropped off into fitful sleep.

The next day the British Embassy was as deserted as ever. The French Embassy, which he found by accident, was the same. There were quite a few tanks about which he assumed were German. Later he learned they were Polish (Warsaw did not fall until 27 September), but 'they fair put the wind up me'. He hung around the Embassy area, keeping out of the way of soldiers and tanks, at a loss as to what to do next, when a Polish girl of his age stopped to ask him, in English, if he was lost. Startled, Len stammered that he was looking for his parents in the Embassy. 'They're gone,' she said, 'I'll take you to my home.'

This was the start of the unreserved hospitality that he experienced throughout his time in Poland. The girl took him to her home, where her mother gave him his first decent meal in days. When her father came home, Len found that he spoke good but formal English. 'I think he must have been a teacher or university professor from the way he talked.' That day and night were terrible, not so much for Len as he was too exhausted to care, but for the Poles. Warsaw was bombed during the day and shelled all through the night. The family slept in the cellar but Len heard nothing.

The following day he was told he must be moved somewhere safer, to Praga, an outer suburb of the city east of the River Vistula. There he was delivered to a cousin's flat for a few days, before being taken to the house of a man he was to know as 'Colonel John'. He had met the man who was to be his mentor and friend throughout the months he was to spend in Poland. It was about 14 September, 1939. Colonel John spoke very good English.

'He told me he was a Polish cavalry officer, but had lived in England for some years. He talked about relatives near Hull, and when he was relaxed he used to tell me about his farm near Lodz, his horses and his dogs. It was sad really, but he was a man of iron.'

It was during his three weeks with 'Colonel John' that Len met an Englishman, Bill Wallace (not his real name), the man who was eventually to get him home many months later.

Wallace seemed totally at home with the Poles, and clearly spoke fluent Polish. Len remembers him as a powerfully-built man in his early forties, just beginning to go grey at the temples, who told him that he was an ICI engineer who had been in Poland for the last six years. Later Len was to realize that he was something more.

A few days later Wallace arrived with two Poles, plus an old truck loaded with vegetables, to retrieve Len's wireless. He clambered into the back and covered himself with a tarpaulin. With the Germans now in occupation they were stopped several times, but not searched. The wireless was where Len had left it, seemingly none the worse for its sojourn in the culvert.

'We got it back to Warsaw, and the Poles went off and came back with about a dozen car batteries. I got the set going, but had no frequencies or callsigns, so I never raised London. After I left Colonel John's house I didn't see the set again.'

Fortunately for Len he was now in the hands of the Polish Resistance. Poland was the first European nation to organize partisan forces to strike back at the Nazis and, in the eastern half of the country from late September, the Soviet occupiers. It was a country whose people were accustomed to guerrilla warfare, a country much occupied and much fought over, much dismembered — situated as it was between Germany and Russia, a country whose forests, mountains and large cities provided ideal terrain for ambushes, surprise attacks, sabotage and assassination. In the autumn of 1939 there was no shortage of weapons or ammunition. The vast army stocks that had been discarded throughout the country, huge quantities of which were secreted away in hundreds of caches, armed the bulk of the Resistance throughout the war. Their principal deficiency was in means of communication. Lack of wireless contact overseas hindered co-ordination. Had Len been able to use his specialist skills to effect, he might have remained in Poland much longer.

He then began a strange itinerant life. For the next few months he moved every few days, sometimes returning to the same house or apartment, sometimes not, but always within the same area. The occupants were all men who came and went without explanation, but middle-aged women used to come in most mornings to clean and prepare food. They were embarrassingly kind to him and, with winter setting in, provided him with woollen underwear and a thick coat. It was to be the only time during the war that he operated without uniform. Had he been caught, he could have been shot without question.

It was a cloistered existence, but a strangely secure one. He grew to trust his companions implicitly. He was not allowed out during the day, so, not having much to do, he turned to hand to helping the women cook. Sometimes in the evenings he was taken out for a walk, usually to some woods near a disused mine about a mile away, but he was always accompanied by at least one Pole.

Although he accepted the necessity for the restrictions on his movements, enforced idleness did not rest comfortably on his shoulders. He admired the men who were continually coming and going on sabotage missions, so he took to doing all he could for them to try to repay their kindness. 'It was not a lot, but I could wash and repair their clothes or make something special for dinner. I even tried my hand at knitting balaclavas when I got some wool.'

One day the alarm was given that a German sweep operation was getting close and Len became the fascinated participant in their immediate reaction drill. In twos and threes, walking fast but not running, the men made for the old mine near which he had been taken on his walks.

'Down inside was an incredible sight. There were dozens of Poles and the place was packed with weapons, ammunition and explosives. There was also quite a collection of German or Russian uniforms.'

From then on every time there was a serious threat Len was taken to the mine, which in effect was the field base of the guerrilla group operating out of Praga.

He was keen to take on a more active role in the nightly sabotage forays. The cooking and washing was useful but boring and, although he could not use his specialist skill, he felt he could contribute in the field. After about two months he was given the chance. With characteristic modesty his description of his role is, 'I really only tagged along. I was given a Russian greatcoat and a fur hat which were much too big so I felt a bit of a fool.'

He was intrigued to see that when a raid was to be made on a German facility the partisans wore Russian uniforms and vice versa. The operations he accompanied were invariably sabotage attacks on the railway yards around Warsaw. Top priority went to disabling the engines. The party of eight to ten men would leave after dark, armed with pistols, sub-machine guns and knives, carrying plenty of explosive and detonators. By devious and varied routes they would make their way towards the target. Normally it was not difficult to avoid the guards or patrols. On his first mission Len was left as lookout with a young Pole of similar age who already had dozens of raids to his credit. From him he learned the first principles of sabotage — always destroy a part that is difficult to replace, or exactly the same piece of every engine or vehicle: 'Like all the left front bogeys so they have a spares problem.'

Len did not go out with every raid, but he participated in about eight operations either as a lookout or carrying explosives. It was in Warsaw that he got his first rudimentary knowledge of demolition. Years later he could see that some operations were a bit disorganized and amateurish (charges sometimes failed to go off) but his admiration for the Poles' courage and dedication was total.

There were, inevitably, reprisals. Men, women, and children were shot, but at the time he did not appreciate the scale of it. The Germans also organized major sweeps to round up able-bodied men for slave labour in Germany or elsewhere. On one occasion he and his friends were down the mine for a week, where his chief concern was the intense cold, before being forced out into the country for three weeks of moving at night from farm to farm. In one refuge he discovered an English book which the farmer gave him. It was Kipling's *Just So Stories*. 'I suppose I must have read it about five times. I can still tell my grandchildren many of them from memory.'

Sometime in March, as the snow started to melt, Bill Wallace received a message from London via the underground that he was to return, bringing Len and another Englishman, Peter Wilson. Len had met Wilson briefly and had been told he was a diver. He seemed a much older and somewhat taciturn individual.

29

Wallace and 'Colonel John' had long discussions on routes. Three other Englishmen, led by a man Len knew as Beecham 'like the pills' were going out by the most commonly used route through Bucharest and Budapest, but Wallace was adamant that he was going via Berlin; he spoke fluent German and good French, and thus was convinced he would have a better chance through Germany and France. Berlin seems to be an extraordinary route to have chosen, but the Poles were a highly organized people and had a number of established courier routes, of which Berlin was one.[9]

They set off in mid-April, taken out of Warsaw by truck, then hiding by day, making their way on foot at night until they got to a large river. The Poles put them across the Oder early one morning by boat, rowing very quietly. Wallace whispered that they were now in Germany. Walking to a small wayside halt, they caught a slow train to a mainline station. Here Wallace bought their tickets, gave them travel documents and told them they would travel in the same compartment but sit apart and not acknowledge each other. To his surprise Len's new passport was American. He spent much of the journey silently rehearsing an American accent.

The express got into Berlin the following evening. It was an eerie feeling being at the heart of Hitler's Third Reich, but life in Berlin in 1940 was much more normal than he had expected.

'Bill seemed to know his way about and took us to a hostel above a newspaper shop which was full of foreign workers. Peter and I were told not to go out. Bill used to go out quite a bit and would bring us food. I can remember a paper he bought with headlines about the German invasion of Holland which he translated for us.'

They were in the hostel for two or three days after which they left Berlin from a different station. Wallace gave them money to buy their own tickets, but Len's nerve failed him. There was a long queue at the ticket office and the police were checking papers. He saw a German officer and, adopting what he fondly hoped was an American accent, he asked him if he spoke English.

'I told him I was trying to rejoin my parents in France and didn't know how to buy a ticket. He spoke perfect English and told me he had been to Oxford. He bought the ticket for me, then took me into his compartment. Funnily enough I felt quite safe with him. He even gave me breakfast next morning in Düsseldorf. Bill gave me a blasting later on.'

They made their way by stages, by train or bus, to near the Belgian border where they crossed the bridge on foot. On the Belgian side Wallace had a heated argument with the Frontier Police and it was some time before they were allowed through.

'Bill was obviously worried — the first time I'd seen him that way. We set off down the road, and as soon as we were out of sight, dodged into a wood where he left Peter and me.'

Wallace was away for at least two hours, by which time Len was desperate. He returned with a solemn-faced Belgian policeman who told them not to move and not to speak to anyone as their papers were not valid for Belgium. Apparently all English speakers were being picked up by the Field Police. After dark the policeman came back and led them for several miles across country to a farm where they were hidden in a hayloft. After that they were on an organized escape route. Passed from hand to hand, moving always at night, sometimes by car, sometimes by bicycle, sometimes by farm cart, but more often on foot, they worked their way through France to the Pyrenees. His main recollection of those weeks is of feeling like a hunted animal, disorientated, exhausted, hungry and frightened. But Wallace kept him going.

'He was an amazing man; except for the Belgian border, always cheerful. I would not have made it but for him. When we crossed the Pyrenees he virtually carried me the last bit over the top.'

In Spain they were arrested and gaoled, which depressed Len considerably. Wallace, however, remained as cheerful as ever, telling them that 'someone from ICI' would arrive shortly to get them out. Sure enough a few days later two Englishmen in civilian clothes appeared. Not long afterwards they were in a car heading for Gibraltar, where Len was separated from the other two and taken to an Army barracks.

His interrogation by the British was unpleasant; initially by a Colonel he remembers as Buchanan, then, over three or four days, by a variety of officers. They did not believe his story. Nor would they let him see Wallace.

'At the time it seemed a hell of a way to be treated by your own side, but now I know how necessary it was.'

Finally he was told his vetting was over and he would be sent back to England. He was given a uniform, reunited with Wallace and Wilson, after which all three were taken to see the Governor.

'He was an impressive man in highly polished riding boots, but didn't say much. He congratulated us on our escape, shook our hands, and next day we were put on board a destroyer bound for Portsmouth.'

Back in London in July Len was interviewed at the War Office, but was surprised how few questions were asked. Only one thing was repeated again and again: if asked where he had been he was to say Scotland. Once satisfied that he had got the message he was given an advance of pay, ration cards and a leave warrant, and told to report to War Office Signals in Regent's Park at the end of his leave.

Len asked about Wallace, as he had not had an opportunity to say goodbye to him in Portsmouth. But the officer told him that Wallace was a civilian so he did not know his whereabouts. He was to meet Wallace only once more, in 1955. A letter from him reached Len in Malaya by a circuitous route. It had no address, just a Tottenham telephone number. On his return to England Len telephoned and they met in a cafe near Sloane Square, an interesting but depressing meeting with, 'a very old and disillusioned Bill' who had had his book on their escape turned down flat by the Foreign Office.

'He said he would keep in touch, but I never heard from him again. He'll be dead by now, I expect.'

The FCO have never heard of Wallace.

CHAPTER THREE

A TASTE OF EXCELLENCE

'I saluted and turned to go, but Captain Stirling called me back. "That wasn't a very good salute. You'll have to do better if you want to join us."'

Apart from his grilling in Gibraltar, where his interrogators initially seemed to view him as an enemy agent, Len was never debriefed on his months in Poland. He was merely told to keep his mouth shut about it, and to insist he had spent the time in Scotland. On leave in London he first found his elder sister Yvonne, who worked in Eaton Place. She describes his sudden appearance as, 'Typical Len, he just walked in off the street and said, "Hello Sis," as if I'd seen him yesterday. He didn't look much different; a bit thinner perhaps. I asked him where he had been and he just said up in Scotland and changed the subject.'[1] That occasion was to prove a momentous one in Len's life. 'Working there with Yvonne was another girl called Connie. I rather liked the look of her.'

Posted to the London Area Signals Regiment, Len was in for almost twelve months of tedium, leading a troglodyte existence as a signaller with the War Office signal unit in an underground bunker at the Whitehall end of St James's Park. Week after week, month after month, the twelve-hour shifts dragged on and on. Sometimes he was on the day shift, sometimes the night, although it made no difference, working as he was under glaring electric lights, what the weather was like or what the time was outside. London was bombed and burning above him as he and his fellow-operators transmitted and received thousands of signals to and from countries and commands all over the world. Although his professional skill as an operator was enhanced to the point of excellence, with morse becoming almost his first language, Lance-Corporal Willmott was bored. As the Battle of Britain was fought and won in the skies above him, as 1941 brought the excitement of General O'Connor's lightning advance against the Italians in the Western Desert, Len languished and fretted in his London bunker. In March of that year he lost his lance-corporal's stripe, which he had received after his return from Poland, for sleeping on guard duty.[2] It was some months before he got it back.

He applied for a posting to the Middle East which was "where the action was". The rejection was curt and cruel: 'Too young and lacks experience.' It was the practice of the operators from the Park to spend their short shift-breaks getting a breath of air by walking up Whitehall and back through Admiralty Arch. On one such walk Len spotted one of the officers who had interviewed him back in 1938. He saluted smartly and said, 'Hello Sir'. The officer asked how he was doing and he seized the chance to say that he was thoroughly brassed off and had had an application for an overseas active service posting turned down. The officer said he would see what he could do. Several weeks later his squadron commander told him he had been summoned to 64 Baker Street for an interview. He was to be vetted by an organization called the Inter-Services Research Bureau (ISRB).

Although unaware of the fact, he was about to join SOE which had been officially established under great secrecy about a year earlier. Special Operations Executive was not the name used by officialdom and Len was unaware that he had worked directly for SOE until after the war; it never appeared on his Service Record. On that document he was posted to MOI(SP). SOE was different things to different people. It was ISRB, it was the Joint Technical Board, or it was the Headquarters Special Training Schools. The War Office referred to it as MOI(SP), while the Admiralty called it NID(Q) and the Air Ministry A1–10.[3] Nobody outside and, like Len, few inside, knew precisely with whom they were dealing.

At his interview in Baker Street two officers probed his knowledge of signals for the best part of an hour. What types of sets could he use? There were detailed technical questions on morse codes and skywave aerials, but no mention of Poland. Len kept quiet on this as the questioners 'seemed to know about me'. He assumed that he would be working for the ISRB, and that it had been behind his escapades in Germany and Poland. He was not to know that ISRB (SOE) had not been formed until he was just finishing his journey home.

Two weeks later a War Office posting order arrived. Lance-Corporal Willmott was going to Force 133 in the Middle East. He was delighted. Back at Baker Street he learned more. He would be joining a special force involved in guerrilla warfare; it would be dangerous, and he must discuss it with nobody. Did he still wish to volunteer? There was no hint of hesitation in his reply. Then another surprise — he was told to put up sergeant's stripes, take forty-eight hours' leave and report to the RTO (Railway Transport Officer) at Euston Station. Len was ecstatic. He was to join a secret special force in the Middle East where the war was hotting up — and he was a sergeant at nineteen! The only problem was that he could tell nobody his good news; even Connie's curiosity as she sewed on his chevrons could not be satisfied.

He had been recruited as a wireless operator for the ill-fated YAK mission.[4] It had been raised, and was commanded by, the traveller and author Peter Fleming, brother of Ian Fleming of James Bond fame. Peter Fleming was then on secondment to SOE from MI-6, and his YAK activities came under Force 133 which was the cover name for SOE in the Middle East. A tangled web indeed. YAK was designed to turn and train Italian prisoners of war who were opposed to fascism for operations back in Italy. Their first and only operation was a disaster with heavy casualties. The unit was disbanded and the survivors posted to SOE's newly-formed Special Training School near Haifa (102STS).[5] These events occurred while Len was on the troopship crawling slowly round Africa, so his final destination was switched to Haifa.

Although he was not to appreciate it until many years later Len had been recruited to SOE without undergoing the usual stringent selection process. By 1941 the interviewing procedures were far more stringent than any he had attended. Success at the interview led to a series of courses designed to sift out the unsuitable, and at the same time give every individual specialist training designed to equip him for the strain of operating in lonely circumstances behind enemy lines. The initial course was in physical fitness, map reading and weapon training. This was followed by four weeks in Scotland at Arisaig on the western coast of Inverness-shire. Here para-military skills had priority. The range of weapons taught was extensive, with emphasis on German and Italian pistols, rifles, and sub-machine guns. Pupils were taught to fire twice at a target with the pistol. It was the start of the now well-known 'double tap' SAS method of recent times. Killing silently with a knife and unarmed combat featured prominently. Demolition training was included, as was railway sabotage, how to set up an ambush, storm a house and the basic infantry tactics of fire and movement.[6]

Those who succeeded in these Group A courses, as they were called, progressed to Group B. These were also set up in country houses such as Beaulieu Manor in the New Forest. Here the teaching was more defensive; learning how the enemy security forces worked, how to avoid detection, how to resist interrogation. Then came more technical aspects; parachuting, clandestine printing, lock or safe breaking, secret wireless techniques and special sabotage. At Brickendon Manor, near Hertford, trainees learned to tell at a glance how to bring a factory to a prolonged halt with the judicious use of a few ounces of explosive.

Len of course knew his signals, had some rudimentary knowledge of explosives, and had fallen off the wings of a bi-plane eight times. The authorities obviously considered that his experience in Poland made up for lack of more formal and varied training. At Euston he joined a draft of three, all Royal Signals sergeants, bound for a troopship at Liverpool. He was dwarfed by his companions: 'I was a midget beside the other two, and they burst out laughing when we met, but we became good friends.' Tom Nolan was a wartime soldier, older than Len and at least 6′ 3″ tall, with a build to match, and 'did he like his beer? With booze under his belt he could be a dangerous man to face in a fight.' The second sergeant, Ranzau, had a shock of ginger hair and the nickname 'Red', but Len was to find him quiet and slow to anger. Although he also topped six feet he was thinner than Nolan, and a pre-war Regular with wartime service in the irregular Lovat Scouts.

During the long voyage around the Cape, apart from some instinctive 'double tap' pistol training and unarmed combat instruction from a former Shanghai policeman called Major Grant-Taylor, three events remain in Len's mind. The first was the gale in the Bay of Biscay. It was a monstrous storm, far worse than anything he had experienced in the *Dove*. But it was the sight of the battleship that was part of the convoy escort that was unforgettable.

'I'd seen some gales off Iceland but I'd never seen anything like this one. This enormous battleship would just disappear from sight, then come surging up like some prehistoric monster with solid water cascading down her decks and over her guns. It was awe-inspiring.'

Shortly after the storm came the second incident, when volunteers were called for to help clean up the mess in the holds where cargo had broken loose.

'Tom Nolan was the first to go down. When he came back he was as pissed as a newt. What the ship's officers had failed to realize was that one part of the hold was full of broken bottles of whisky and, trust Tom, he'd made the most of it.'

Thereafter time below was strictly limited. Even so Len, whose stomach was totally unmoved, watched with amusement as the volunteers came up 'swaying all over the place and as sick as parrots from whisky fumes and the ship's motion.'

The third event was altogether more serious. The alarm bells went in the middle of the night and everybody scrambled to action stations at the prospect of a U-boat attack. The ship increased speed, then started a zigzag course. A number of explosions were heard which momentarily lit up the darkness on the horizon. It was a miserable night spent huddled in greatcoats and life jackets. With his trawler experience Len 'shuddered for the poor bastards that had been torpedoed'. In the morning the convoy had vanished and they steamed southwards alone.

In Cairo the three sergeants reported to the famous Rustum Buildings which housed the headquarters of SOE. It struck them as a chaotic place. Len was not impressed with his reception, particularly in the attitude of some of the senior officers towards the NCOs. There were about a dozen new arrivals and their briefing was carried out by a major in the Cameron Highlanders. According to Len he was 'an obnoxious lah-de-dah bastard who treated the sergeants like dirt.'[7] There is little doubt that the senior NCOs, who were all specialist instructors in their own field, were mishandled at the outset, messed about and told the bare minimum. Several, including Len, came to the brink of packing it in but stuck it out because of their pending move to Haifa and the fact that Grant-Taylor's training on the ship had whetted their appetites for unconventional operations.

Within a week or so they moved by train to the newly formed 102STS on Mount Carmel, near Haifa. Another briefing followed their arrival. This time it was the Commandant, 'a laid-back toff who didn't seem real'. Initially Len and his two comrades were the only NCO instructors at the school. They were pitched into a tight training schedule from the outset as the first batch of partisans had already arrived. Len was a wireless instructor with a mixed bunch of Greeks, Yugoslavs and a few Italians.

'We had these blokes for four to six weeks. It was our job to teach them how to operate what sets we had, and a pretty primitive lot they were, even including the old No. 1 set I had been taught at Catterick as a boy.'

After about six weeks at Mount Carmel Len was summoned to the Commandant's office. He had not seen much of the aristocratic, casual Colonel who commanded the School, but had been advised not to underestimate him. 'I understand you have jumped out of aeroplanes,' drawled the Commandant in a voice suggesting mild distaste. Len paused before answering for, as far as he knew, his 1938 parachute course was not in his Army records. He replied cautiously, 'Yes, Sir, but I never got my wings'. The Colonel waved dismissively. An old schoolfriend of his had just started a new unit in the Delta and needed a parachute instructor until properly qualified people arrived from England; 'So be a good chap and get yourself to Kabrit to help out.'

It seemed inappropriate to argue or to point out that he had merely leapt off the wings of a bi-plane three years before, and was in no way qualified to instruct. Once more Len accepted his new assignment without comment or question. He had no idea where Kabrit was, or that he was to meet the embryo unit from which the SAS was to emerge.

Kabrit is eighty miles east of Cairo. It was mid-October, 1941, and 'L' Detachment of the non-existent 1st Special Air Service Brigade had been formed for only a few weeks. Len is remembered as 'the little bloke who looked about fourteen who turned up wearing sergeant's stripes and no wings'.[8] If some thought he appeared insignificant, he himself was greatly impressed with what he saw. What struck him instantly was the contrast in how the officers talked to — and treated — the NCOs, instead of ignoring them as at Haifa.

He was met at the station by a tall, gangling Lieutenant with long blond hair driving a jeep, who seemed genuinely delighted to see him. Len was agreeably surprised by his opening remark, 'It's very good of you to come down.'

The first evening opened his eyes even wider. Used to the strict divide between officers and other ranks, he was astounded to find a number of officers in the Sergeants' Mess discussing training methods, parachuting, equipment, weapons, and generally swapping stories. From time to time troopers came in, were offered a beer and joined whatever discussion was going on. Opinions were freely traded as among equals with points of view strongly argued or defended, quite regardless of rank. It was difficult to know who was who, as nobody wore badges of rank.

The camp had a purposeful air about it, well laid out, immaculately tidy, with the messes comfortably furnished. Just how they had come to be so comfortably furnished he did not learn for a week or two. The story is part of SAS legend, and bears repeating for those who may have forgotten or not heard about this early example of SAS self-help.[9]

Denied even the most rudimentary comforts — according to authority they were not available — the fledgling SAS just happened on an adjacent camp with its occupants, a New Zealand battalion, temporarily absent on a desert exercise. On the presumption that anything going missing would be blamed on light-fingered Egyptians, and that the New Zealanders would obtain replacements very rapidly, everything from beds to brooms — even a piano — were transferred in the course of one night.

L Detachment, 1st Special Air Service Brigade, was the brainchild of a twenty-four-year-old Scots Guards Captain, scion of an ancient Scottish family. David Stirling had been serving in the Guards Commando, part of an ad hoc force under Brigadier Laycock, designed to harry the enemy by seaborne landings behind enemy lines. Stirling was not impressed. A giant of a man at 6' 5", he had an enquiring and independent mind; he has since been described as a man who had twelve brilliant ideas a year of which eleven were impractical and the twelfth ahead of its time.[10] To Stirling the whole concept of Layforce was wrong. Attacks on the enemy rear were always from the sea — right hook — and therefore predictable; far too many men were involved with too many sergeants shouting, 'Fall in by your right'.

After several operations, including the abortive raid on Rommel's headquarters where Lieutenant-Colonel Lord Keyes was killed and won a posthumous VC, Stirling was convinced that something different was needed. He advocated small, carefully selected and highly trained teams capable of being inserted by land, sea, or air, totally self-contained and operating behind enemy lines for weeks, even months. The first priority was to obtain parachutes. By chance, a brother officer, an Australian and Cambridge rugger Blue, came across a consignment of parachutes destined for India, but unloaded accidentally in Egypt. They were acquired. On his third training jump Stirling's parachute did not open properly. He hit the desert hard, severely damaging his back. In hospital he put his ideas on paper, and the story of his climbing the fence at GHQ Middle East in order to put them across in high places, and being pursued round the corridors until he took refuge in the chief-of-staff's office has been told many times. Unconventional though his approach had been, the C-in-C Middle East, General Sir Claude Auchinleck, gave him permission to raise L Detachment.[11]

Farsighted as the General proved, he could not have envisaged that by the end of the war there would be five SAS regiments; two British, two French and one Belgian. Even Stirling could not have foreseen, fifty years on, that the letters SAS would be synonymous with the élite of élite troops, and the coveted winged dagger worn by similar units of the French, Belgian, Greek, Dutch, Australian, New Zealand, Rhodesian and Indian special force units.

Len was interviewed first by the young Lieutenant who had met him, then briefly by the Adjutant, and finally by Captain Stirling who surprised Len by thanking him for volunteering to help with the parachute training. Then, in a conversational tone, he asked, 'I gather you would like to join us?'

After that Len was subjected to almost an hour of penetrating questions. What did he know about tactics or demolitions? Could he drive? What were his radio skills? What distances had he operated over? How fit was he? He was a bit small but could he carry heavy packs? All this time Stirling remained absolutely still, crouched forward over the table, gripping the front edge. His eyes never left Len's.

Disconcerted by the unflinching gaze, Len did not feel his answers were particularly convincing, so he was agreeably pleased when Stirling leaned back in his chair, stretched his arms above his head, and said, 'OK, you'll have to pass the full course and convince the others you are up to it. We'll give you a try when the para team arrives and has settled in.' Len saluted and turned to go, but Captain Stirling called him back. 'That wasn't a very good salute,' he said quietly, 'You'll have to do better if you want to join us.'

Parachuting was to be Len's speciality with L Detachment, so he set about learning from one of the RAF sergeants, putting in as many jumps as he could, sometimes four or five a day. Although the techniques and technicalities of parachuting had advanced considerably since his first jump, they were still quite primitive compared with today. At least all the jumpers used the static line method, and the aircraft had either a hole in the floor or a door for exiting, rather than falling off a wing. Nevertheless, it was a frightening, for some even terrifying, experience. That year, 1941, at the parachute school at Ringway in England a former SOE agent's comments sum up the situation graphically:

'The percentage of accidents, at that time about five in a thousand, seemed to us relatively disquieting. . . .Hardly had we arrived when we were taken out to the airfield "to give us confidence". We watched sandbags being parachuted; a good half of the parachutes did not open, and the bags thudded into the ground with a dull, flat noise that brought us no confidence at all. We looked at each other, rather pale. Still, after all, some parachutes had managed to open; so we might be lucky.'[12]

This demonstration turned out to be more than necessarily pessimistic. After the war it was calculated that about 1,350 agents had parachuted into France, each having averaged four jumps, with only six fatalities, a rate of around one in 900 descents, an encouraging improvement, although not enough to dispel the fear from an entirely unnatural activity.

Len had to learn the use of the static line. The parachute was attached to a strong point, usually a steel rail inside the aircraft, by a length of material known as the static line. The other end was fixed to the parachute pack by a series of progressively stronger ties. When the man jumped the pack containing the canopy and rigging lines was broken from his back by these ties, and hung from the aircraft. As he fell the rigging lines were dragged from his pack, so by the time the canopy appeared the man was the length of the rigging lines — twenty feet — below. A final tie, holding the apex of the canopy to the pack, then broke and the parachute was fully extended, ready to open, leaving the pack and static line attached to the aircraft. Because it was all automatic, with the parachutist no longer having to judge when to pull a ripcord, jumping from a much lower height was entirely practical. This in turn gave a much shorter time in the air, which enabled greater accuracy for the drop and less vulnerability to groundfire. With a jump from 500 feet, for example, the canopy had only fully opened for a matter of a few seconds before the jumper landed, with a jolt roughly the equivalent of leaping off a fourteen-foot wall.

These improvements were not foolproof, as Len himself witnessed at Kabrit. One morning, after making two or three jumps, he, along with

Captain Stirling, was watching further trials from a Bombay aircraft which had a side door through which to exit. Inside the aircraft twelve men were waiting their turn under the eye of the sergeant dispatcher positioned by the door. It was his job to hook up each man's static line to the rail, check it and show the jumper all was ready. This was done. All saw the red light flash on — the two-minutes-to-go signal. The leading man shuffled forward, eyes glued to the light and on the dispatcher's raised arm. Then the green light. The first man leapt from the door as the sergeant's arm came down. However, as the sergeant yelled 'Go', he saw to his horror the ring break away from the clip which was attached to the rail. The static line disappeared out of the aircraft after the jumper, who plummeted to his death a few seconds later. Before the dispatcher could prevent him, the next man had gone through the door as well. The same thing happened. The sergeant screamed a warning and grabbed the third man. Inside was an atmosphere of numbed disbelief and shock.

Stirling cancelled the rest of the trials but announced they should be ready to go again at 5.30 a.m. the next day. Careful examination discovered the fault. Pressure from the slipstream had twisted the ring hard against the clip to such an extent that it opened to release the ring. Alternative clips were available. The following morning Stirling was the first man to jump. There were no more accidents. Some months later he was to discover that Ringway had had a similar fatality, but the cause had not been circulated.

Like most parachutists Len enjoyed the exhilaration of the descent once he had heard the comforting crack of the canopy open above him. Beforehand, the anticipation inside the aircraft was always scaring, no matter how many times he jumped. During his career he was to make 497 descents, of which five were behind enemy lines and a number into the Malayan jungle. In 1959 someone suggested he make three more to give him the magical 500. He declined. Although something of a fatalist, 'I saw no point in jumping just to ring up the numbers.'

Parachute training was still in its infancy in 1941, particularly at Kabrit. There was a lot of trial and error, improvisation and discussion. Len was much impressed by the latter. It stemmed from the SAS's pursuit of excellence which was Stirling's overriding principle from the outset. It took, and still takes, the form of a tireless and penetrating attention to detail, a thorough examination of everything they did. Nothing was perfect; everything could be done better. A recent example was the superbly successful assault on the Iranian Embassy in London. Within an hour of the operation the SAS were analysing every aspect to ensure a better result next time.

Len was soon drawn into the discussions about parachute training. Every drill, every jump, every exercise was dissected in detail. Len relates an example of how the SAS worked in the early days. It was a typical evening

41

in the Sergeants' Mess. One of the officers came over and said, 'Look Len [he was getting used to the SAS habit of calling NCOs and men by their Christian names], we only get ten into a Whitley, why can't we have twelve, that is, three four-man patrols?' To get twelve parachutists in, Len explained, they would have to do without two of the three dispatchers. In those days there was one dispatcher at the forward end of the cabin checking harnesses and parachutes, one at the other end checking static lines, and the third at the hole in the floor or at the door seeing the parachutists out of the plane. Even then, Len said, 'You'll be pushed for space with two extra fully-kitted men.'

'Why are they necessary?' was the retort. 'We know what we are doing now, so why can't we do our own checks and just keep the dispatcher at the hole?' The pros and cons were argued back and forth with a number of others joining in, the forerunner of what the SAS today call a 'Chinese parliament'; everyone has their say from troopers upwards, but the boss's decision is final. Eventually the officer said, 'Right, that's settled then. You fix it with the RAF, and we'll try it tomorrow.'

The four-man patrol, or 'brick' as it is now called, has stood the test of time and remains the basic tactical sub-unit of the SAS over fifty years later. Why four and not three or five? The usual reason given is that three cannot carry enough, while five men behave like a conventional infantry section — one man in command, the remainder heads down and arse up.[13] Each brick contained a demolitions expert, a highly-skilled long-distance wireless operator, a medic and the Commander.

Len was too busy on his parachute training to see much of the SAS's other activities, although men pushed to the limits of exhaustion on the many exercises and forced marches became a familiar sight in camp. So too was the mixture of disappointment and relief on the faces of men who had not met Stirling's standards and had not been selected; no one fails SAS selection, even today; most find of their own accord that it is not for them; others are just not selected which leaves no slur on their military ability, and means no more than that they are not suitable for the specialized SAS organization. Nevertheless, he learned the principles laid down by Stirling on which the SAS were to operate.

Ground training also posed problems; how to simulate a landing at speed in order to practise the relaxed roll necessary to avoid ankle or leg injuries. A number of contraptions were invented, including a 'death slide' from makeshift towers with the aspiring parachutist holding two handles attached to a bicycle wheel which rode on a taut, angled wire. Descent was totally uncontrolled, resulting in a large number of accidents, and the towers themselves were inherently unstable.[14] The system was discontinued until a proper parachute training tower could be constructed. Stirling's next idea was to build a sloping ramp with wooden platforms mounted on rollers. When the platforms reached full speed the trainee would jump and roll. Perhaps fortunately, he was defeated by a shortage of wood, so he switched to practising rolling after jumping out of the back of 15-cwt trucks at 30 m.p.h. This, too, added to the casualty list.

One of Len's innovations was to suggest that flat tops be fitted to the trucks so that trainees could jump from the side, jumping forward with the truck as you would from the door of a plane, and simulating the momentum of landing, whether rolling forward or rolling backwards on impact.

When the parachute instructor team of three sergeants arrived, headed by Captain Peter Palmer, Palmer was surprised to see that Len, who had by then done at least forty jumps, was still not wearing wings. He told Len to do five more jumps which would count as his official qualification descents. Within twenty-four hours Len had his wings.

Then disaster struck. Len was demonstrating the technique of jumping from a moving truck to some new arrivals. He jumped first, caught his foot in a pothole, turned over on it and broke his ankle. Palmer personally took him up to the medical reception station in Kabrit. The doctors examined his injury and pronounced that it would require X-ray but that they did not have the necessary facilities. Two days later he was evacuated to the general hospital in Cairo.

The next six weeks were intensely frustrating. With his ankle in plaster he was released on light duties after a couple of weeks. He was billeted in one of the SOE houses at Mena, and initially used as a relief wireless operator at Rustum Buildings. That at least gave him an insight into the difficulties under which the headquarters operators laboured in trying to establish contact with SOE parties in the field, thus making him rather more charitable towards them when he was himself deployed. While there he heard rumours of a calamitous SAS operation in the desert, with many casualties. It was only after the war that he learned the extent of the disaster. Five planes took off on the night of 16 November, 1941, in atrocious conditions of driving rain, low cloud and gale-force winds; one was shot down, another talked down on to a German airfield, and the remainder dropped their troops many miles wide of the DZ. Of the sixty-four officers and men who took part, only twenty-two reached the rendezvous.

To this day Len has a distinct guilt complex that he was not with them. Confident that he would have passed the selection course but for his injury, he feels in some strange way that he should have been on that first operation.

He became engaged in a one-sided battle against the medical and SOE authorities in Cairo to get himself graded fit to return to the SAS. It was a battle he failed to win. With his leg out of plaster he found himself fulfilling the role of courier between Rustum Buildings, GHQ and other parts of SOE

Cairo's empire. He became useful to the staff, so they were even less inclined to let him go.

Cairo was an extraordinary place in November, 1941. Rommel was almost at the gates, rumours were rife, and there was more than a touch of panic everywhere. Moving around on his duties, Len saw a good deal of it and was singularly unimpressed by what he saw. Staffs were burning mountainous piles of paper. There was ash everywhere, with a great pall of smoke hanging over the city. Len was called upon to assist with the Rustum Buildings bonfire. It was utterly depressing. He consoled himself slightly with the thought that if the Germans did overrun Egypt it would provide the opportunity for sabotage operations such as he had seen in Poland, and for which he had started training at Haifa.

It never came to that. Rommel's panzer divisions turned back from their dash for the frontier, while the fighting around Sidi Rezegh east of Tobruk finally produced a stand-off. The British military authorities had regarded it as a touch-and-go situation. Len's records pessimistically show him as 'On special duties pending capture by the Germans.'[15]

Shortly before Christmas, 1941, Len was posted back to 102STS. He was bitterly disappointed at not returning to the SAS as he had been so impressed by their methods and attitude. He mentally resolved he would return to them some day. It was to take him ten years.

Back at Mount Carmel Len was destined for another nine months of the repetitive, short training cycles, aimed at producing effective partisan fighters destined for Greece or Yugoslavia, before he would see action again. He was pleased, however, to renew his friendship with Sergeants Nolan and Ranzau. From the latter, whose service with the Lovat Scouts had taught him demolition techniques, Len gained useful knowledge. His interest in explosives had been aroused during his raids against the railways in Warsaw, so he tapped into Ranzau's expertise as often as possible.

Messing about with explosives can be great fun if you know what you are doing. Properly handled they can add excitement and considerable realism to otherwise tedious training exercises. Len and his fellow instructors determined to enliven the final phases of their programme.

Their concern was that they were training people under peacetime rules and regulations to go back to their own countries to fight for real. To be of lasting value training should be interesting and realistic as well as physically and mentally demanding. The dictum 'more sweat, less blood' has much truth in it.

The advanced part of the wireless training involved going out into the countryside for a week at a time to practise communications in field conditions, operating over long distances. A disused fort, with a self-

H.Q. Force 133,
M.E.F.

B6/602.

24 Jan 44.

Dear Mrs. Willmott,

The King has recently approved the award of the M.M. to your son, Sjt. Willmott, in recognition of his gallant and distinguished service during operations against the enemy.

As he is unable to write himself, owing to the military situation, I thought you would like to know the good work he has been, and is still, doing, and that he is very fit.

Would you please note that all mail for him should in future be sent to the above address.

6. "For three years he had been a sergeant, much of it on active service behind enemy lines, for which he had been awarded the BEM and MM" (p.83). Letters to Len's mother and father informing them of his awards.

HQ Force 133,
M.E.F.

B6/602.

1 Mar 44.

Dear Mr. Willmott,

Thank you very much for your kind letter of 6th Feb. I am so glad the information reached you safely.

I have some more good news for you in that your son Sjt. Leonard Willmott, has also received the B.E.M. in recognition of his distinguished services. We have just received official confirmation of this award, and I therefore hasten to pass th information to you.

I hope it will not be too long before you receive some more mail from him again, and better still that he should return home and tell you all about his deeds himself.

Sincerely,

7. "On 22 April, 1944, Len and Connie were married" (p.83).

appointed guardian, an ancient Arab who had served in Glubb Pasha's Arab Legion, provided a useful base. But before they could use it they had always to inspect the old man. Proudly, this grizzled ancient would turn out in bleached and patched but immaculate uniform.

'He had a Martini-Henry rifle even older than himself, and you could have shaved in the stock. Everything, but everything polishable was polished till it gleamed; boots, belt, bandolier, every round of his meagre arsenal of ammunition. We used to wonder what would happen if he fired his musket, but decided not to put it to the test.'

Honour satisfied, the old man would squat in the shade to watch with interest what went on. He allowed no one anywhere near the fort, and gave the sergeants ample warning if any officers from the school came too close.

A series of exercise tests was devised to make the training realistic. Trainees were divided up into groups by their nationalities to encourage a lively competitive spirit. Arduous cross-country marches, being hunted by others, concealment of their sets and aerials and, a favourite of the ancient Arab, clearing the fort of booby traps. He would cackle with glee when a puff-charge went off. Len's comment was, 'We had to watch it a bit, as they sometimes got carried away with the Greeks hell bent on murdering the Yugoslavs and vice versa, but nobody got seriously hurt.'

Not satisfied with that they decided on something more ambitious, a raid on the Mount Carmel camp, with themselves as guerrilla leaders.

'Tom decided to go for the officers' mess silver which, quite incidentally, was kept with their booze supplies. Red wanted the CO's jeep, and I decided to capture the master cook's pet pig — a bloody animal which got better fed than we did.'

Knowing that the other two planned to cut the perimeter fence, Len decided on the bold course: straight through the main gate. The camp was guarded by West African troops: 'great big black cheerful bastards, but as thick as three planks.' As he had been out for a week Len did not know the current password, but at the gate said to the sentry, 'I'm Sergeant Willmott; you know me.'

'Yes, Sah,' was the reply with a flashing display of white teeth, 'Ah knows you is Sergeant Willmott, but you don't know de passaword so you go in de clink.'

Len decided against arguing with sixteen stone of African soldier with a fixed bayonet and allowed himself to be prodded into the presence of the guard corporal, an even bigger African who looked like Idi Amin. In the guardroom the password was negotiated for the promise of a bottle of whisky. Thereafter it was plain sailing — at least initially.

'The pig gave no trouble. It was all bedded down for the night, so we stuffed it into a sack and put in in the back of the truck. I told the trainees to sing to drown its squeals. I got hold of a bottle of whisky and the corporal shouted something like, "You be careful in de town. All de girls got pox".'

Next morning all hell erupted in camp. The African corporal, totally intoxicated, swore blind that he had seen no one, while the master cook went berserk over the loss of his pig. As there were patrols out combing the nearby area, the three sergeants decided to lie low for twenty-four hours, then return their trophies the following night. By this time the pig was getting restive and loudly rejecting the rations offered to it. Also its smell was making its presence noticeable over a wide area.

'Red and Tom went off with one of the trucks and the CO's jeep, relying on some cock-and-bull story about finding it abandoned in the desert and the silver in it. I was to follow later and try to return the pig. Then my bloody truck broke down.'

They were twenty miles from camp with the pig more than restive and none of the trainees willing to go near it. It was left to Len. 'Try carrying a half-grown porker in your arms; it's just not on.' He found the ancient Arab and tried to hire his donkey. Spotting the pig, the old man called down all the curses of Allah on their heads before taking off into the night, abandoning even his precious rifle. 'I didn't know then that the pig is an unclean animal to Mohammedans.'

Inevitably the pig got out of the sack and a hilarious chase round the inside of the fort ensued until it was recaptured. By then Len had had enough, so got one of the Greeks, who was a butcher by trade, to kill it. 'We had a smashing barbecue, though some of the trainees found they couldn't eat a pig they had got to know so personally.'

The Commandant had a sense of humour and admired initiative, so retribution was less severe than it might have been. It cost Len the price of another pig and two bottles of whisky to mollify the master cook.

There were periodic visits to SOE Cairo to be briefed on signals developments which allowed the by now notorious trio to sample some of the city's fleshpots. On one of their earlier trips they made a grand tour of the bars. Three somewhat unsteady sergeants later hailed a taxi but could not find the building where they were billeted. Driving round in circles they found the large, high-fenced communications centre that they knew was near their destination. Spotting a patrolling sentry they paid off the taxi and climbed over the fence to ask the way.

> 'When the sentry saw us he fainted — literally. Tom had a bottle of beer in his pocket so he poured it over this bloke. When he came to he looked as if he had seen three ghosts. All he said was, "Christ! you've walked through the fucking minefield," and passed out again.'

Nolan appears to have been the ringleader on these expeditions, and with drink on board was decidedly unpredictable. Coming out of a bar on another Cairo expedition, they came across some New Zealanders disputing the fare with a taxi driver.

> 'Tom barged in, asked where they'd come from, took the money out of one of the Kiwi's hand, paid the driver what he thought was fair and handed the rest back. The Kiwi, instead of being grateful, took a swing at Tom. So Tom laid him out. Some Aussies intervened, so Tom laid out one of them too. In no time there was a good old free-for-all so we grabbed Tom and scarpered.'

Len thought the safest place to take him was Shepheard's Hotel, officially out of bounds to other ranks, but they knew a back way in and had a friend in the barman. 'It was fine if you could avoid the doorman and stayed in the bar.' Unfortunately, on this occasion, one officer took exception to their presence. He was less than polite, telling them to get out. Len and Ranzau got up to leave but Nolan was having none of it. Two other officers then joined in and an embarrassing slanging match ensued.

> 'Tom had clouted all three of them before we could grab him and drag him out through the back. We got him home okay, and he reckoned it had been a great night. He was posted soon afterwards and I never saw him again.'

By mid-1942 the training schedule, which involved repeating the same course over and over again, was beginning to pall. Len formally asked his Squadron Commander for a more active role. He was told his time would come. In late September it did. He was to report to the airfield back at Kabrit immediately.

CHAPTER FOUR

THE RUSHING RIVER

'Operation HARLING was a fundamental cock-up from the start. From what I know now the planning was bloody near criminal. But you've got to remember that I was only a sergeant, and in those days other ranks were told nothing. If I'm a bit harsh about some officers remember it was as I saw it as a 21 year old sergeant at the time. It was years after the war that I heard the full story.'

Operation HARLING was the codename given by SOE in Cairo to the mission to destroy the railway line that wriggled its way south through the mountains and defiles of Greece. It was a major German supply route, whose destination was the port of Athens at Piræus from where war materials were shipped through the Greek islands to Rommel in North Africa. Among the precipitous mountain ranges of Roumeli and Attica this track crossed three viaducts, two called after the rivers they crossed: the Gorgopotamos (rushing river), and the Papadia (priest's wife), while the third was the Asopos.[1] If any of these could be dropped into the water it would cut the enemy's lines of communications in this area for weeks, perhaps months. It was, so the staff considered, an ideal task for guerrillas. On 4 September, 1942, SOE Cairo sent a coded message to the partisan co-ordinator in Athens asking if one of the small bands of *andarte* (partisans) could blow up the Papadia viaduct. They wanted the job done quickly so that vital supplies might be denied to the Germans on the eve of General Montgomery's crucial battle at El Alamein that was then being planned.[2]

Not until 21 September did a reply arrive. To destroy any of the viaducts in the Mount Giona area the *andartes* would need substantial support. Specifically at least ten British advisers, including two sabotage experts plus the explosives, were needed. To complicate matters further the men and equipment would need to drop between 28 September and 3 October. That left a week to cobble together this critical operation. The first problem was to find a commander.

On 20 September Colonel Eddie Myers, a Royal Engineer Colonel who was due to return to the UK in two weeks after seven years in the Middle East, was visited by a Lieutenant-Colonel Hamilton, an SOE staff officer.

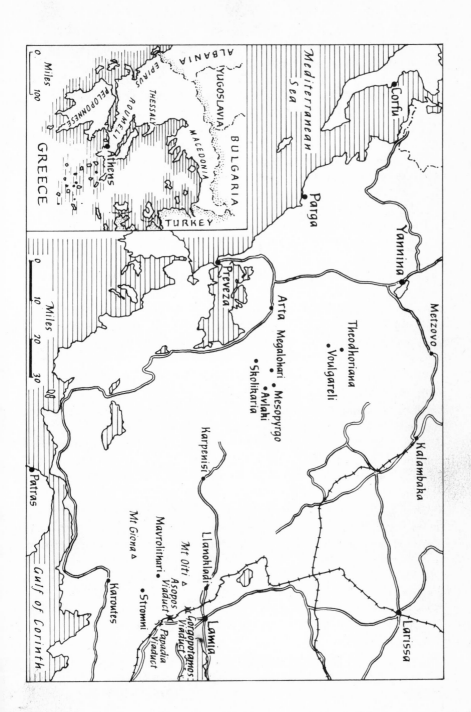

Mediterranean Sea

Corfu

Parga

Yannina

Metzovo

Preveza

Arta

Theodhoriana

Megalohari • Voulgareli

Mesopyrgo

Aviahi

Skoluikaria

Kalambaka

Karpenisi

Llanokladi

Mt Otti ▲

Mavrolithari •

Mt Giona ▲

Asopos Viaduct

Gorgopotamos Viaduct

Papadia Viaduct

Stromni

Lamia

Larissa

Karoutes

Patras

Gulf of Corinth

0 10 20 30 40
Miles

ALBANIA
YUGOSLAVIA
EPIRUS
MACEDONIA
BULGARIA
THESSALY
ROUMELI
PELOPONNESE
Athens
TURKEY

GREECE

0 100
Miles

49

He was looking for engineer officers with parachute training to volunteer for a bridge-blowing operation behind enemy lines in Greece. Spotting the parachute wings on Myers' uniform Hamilton not too subtly remarked, 'I see you're a parachutist.' Myers' protestations that he spoke no Greek, was a regular soldier untrained in guerrilla warfare, was due to return to the UK, was unfit, had not done a proper parachute course, and anyway did not want the job, were gently undermined with the words, 'But that doesn't matter a bit! You are just the sort of chap we are looking for. How would you like to take command of this show? It's frightfully important. You would be back in a few weeks, and you could then go home on the crest of a wave.' Over the next day or so more pressure and persuasion were exerted. On 23 September Myers found he had accepted the job.[3]

A few days earlier Major The Hon C. M. Woodhouse, who had experience of Greece and was already working for SOE, was waylaid in Cairo *en route* to join Stirling's SAS. He was simply asked, 'Would you be willing to be parachuted into Greece next week?'[4] As he could think of no good reason to say 'no', he said 'yes'. He was to be second-in-command to Myers.

Myers had five days to get ready; five days in which to select and assemble the teams, plan how they were to deploy and operate, collect together the equipment, wireless sets, arms and explosives, and obtain the necessary aircraft. In the event, several of those chosen had to do their first parachute jumps two days prior to the operation.

In outline all Myers knew was that he was to drop into Greece, meet up with the *andarte*, blow at least one viaduct and then get out, leaving only a small party behind with the Greek partisans. Speed was of the essence with the railway track needing to be destroyed quickly (the Allied attack at Alamein started on 23 October). In theory it was just possible; in practice the timing was out by just over a month. Fortunately drawings of the Papadia and Gorgopotamos viaducts were available, while those for Asopos were due to be flown from London within a day or so.[5]

The plan that eventually emerged was for three Liberators, as the only aircraft with the range available, each to take a team of four. Myers and a second team would drop in the area of Mount Giona, while the third team under Woodhouse dropped about thirty miles north-west of Giona in central Greece where they had been asked to link up with a prominent *andarte* leader called Zervas. They would all go on the night of 28 September. None of this meagre information was passed down to Len and his two sergeant signaller companions, nor to the other officers, as Len discovered forty years later.

Len arrived at Kabrit airfield just two days before take-off. He was far from impressed by his reception, although he was delighted to meet Doug Phillips, another ex-boy whom he knew from Catterick. Neither had any idea where they were going. With hindsight Len's judgement of the teams was harsh, but in 1942 he was a rather 'bolshie' young sergeant.

'Team No. 1 consisted of Colonel Myers, a sapper, small, dead regimental, a hunting type stuffed-shirt pre-war officer, and much too old in my view (he was 38); Captain Denys Hamson, a commando who I thought was a Riviera playboy type; Captain Tom Barnes, a tough New Zealand sapper and the best of the lot — he could talk to the sergeants; and me as signaller, although I had no idea why I had been picked. I only met Myers at the airfield.

'Team 2 was Major "Monty" Woodhouse, good-looking, very much the toff, self-assured but distant; Captain Arthur Edmonds, another Kiwi sapper and a good bloke but much quieter than Barnes; Captain Nat Barker, another commando who I thought was also a playboy type. He knew a lot about horses (he had run a stud-farm in Thessaly pre-war) but hopeless with mules in Greece; and Sergeant Mike Chitis, the Rumanian Jew.

'Team 3 was led by Major John Cook, another commando who I thought bloody useless from the start — in fact Myers demoted him later in Greece; Captain Themos Marinos, the only Greek, but he knew what he was on and proved tough with the *andarte*; this little half-Indian bloke, Lieutenant Inder Gill,[6] who looked about fourteen, but I quite took to him later; and Sergeant Doug Phillips, my mate from Catterick who got himself killed later trying to prove himself . . . bloody waste.'

On the airfield, just prior to boarding, Len had his first sight of his wireless and the new system of parachuting with either the set or batteries suspended above the operator's head. He was not reassured.

'Anyway, two days after I arrived in Kabrit I found myself in the back of a Liberator bomber, destination Greece. I saw my wireless and batteries for the first time at the airfield, but not all the ancillary equipment like headphones, crystals, charging engine etc.; of all bloody stupid things, these had been packed in containers to be dropped separately. The wireless was the new SOE suitcase set, the B1, which I had never seen before. There was no instruction book and no opportunity to test it. The batteries were charged but drained of their acid for the drop. There was acid in the containers — so we were told.

Then the final straw. A new harness had been designed for jumping with the wireless and the batteries. The theory was that they had to be dropped with the same care as the bodies. Bloody marvellous. One or the other was suspended above your head. Myers took the wireless, I took the batteries. I didn't like it, but there was nothing I could do about it.'

Everybody had to haul themselves into the aircraft through the hole in the floor from which they would later make their exit, and shuffle forward to crouch in the small space behind the cockpit. It was necessary to have as much weight at the front as possible during take off. Once airborne, all four clambered back past the bomb bays in which all the stores canisters were stowed. There was a five-hour flight ahead of them. Despite the bitter cold Len, as usual, went to sleep.

With about an hour to go before the drop Len was woken by Myers telling the team to get into their jumping overalls and parachute harnesses. The pilot was looking for fires on the ground laid out in the form of a cross, but despite circling several times, flying to the west coast of Greece and back, circling again, he failed to spot anything resembling the signal. Their instructions had been 'No lights, no drop', so there was no option but to return to Cairo. All three aircraft had the same experience. The Liberators could not be readied for another try until the night of 30 September.[7]

The plan for the next try was that, lights or no lights, the drop would be made. If no recognizable signals were seen Major Cook's party would jump first, as near as possible to Mount Giona. If he found it safe he would light red flares to guide the other two groups down.

In the event the second attempt was an exact repeat of the first; no cross of lights, much circling, and a fruitless flight to the west coast and back. There were bonfires below in places, sometimes in pairs but nothing resembling a cross. However, having returned to the Giona area Myers saw three fires in what seemed like a fairly flat valley; the pilot agreed it was a suitable area so the decision was taken to jump. The four men were then crouched around the trap-door-type opening in the floor with static lines hooked up. The Liberator would make two passes over the drop zone; on the first Myers would lead, closely followed by Tom Barnes, the New Zealand sapper. Then the aircraft would make its turn and came back to let Len and the Greek-speaking Hamson jump. The technique was to sit with your feet in the hole facing forward. The moment the green light came on, the jumper pushed himself forward and endeavoured to stand to attention in the centre of the hole. If done properly the likelihood of banging your face against the opposite side of the hole was greatly reduced. Once out, the static line did the rest.

For Myers with the radio and Len with the batteries it was not a pleasant descent. Myers found that the two main supporting straps by which he was suspended from the wireless squeezed painfully against his face. They both found that hanging from the wireless package rather than directly from the parachute meant they swung like a pendulum over which they had no control. This, coupled with a strong wind, meant that choice of a landing spot was impossible. In fact all team members were well scattered, blown over the valleys and hills below at great speed, before coming down into forest-covered mountain sides. Len's comment afterwards was:

'It was as black as pitch. I couldn't see the ground approaching and went crashing through the trees. I could hear the bloody batteries crashing through after me and I remember thinking, If this is curtains, I hope they don't tell Mum I was killed by a bloody battery. I'd landed in a pine forest on a bloody near vertical slope which was all shale. I slid on my arse till I hit a tree which knocked the wind out of me. The batteries had disappeared and I thought, Bugger the Colonel, I've had enough for one night; tied myself to the nearest tree and went to sleep.'

At dawn Len untied himself and slithered down to the edge of the forest to take stock. He was on one side of a V-shaped, heavily wooded ravine. A small village was just visible about half a mile away, but there was no sign of the others. They could be anywhere in that wind and, in those forest and mountains, quite possibly injured.

Hamson may not have been Len's favourite officer, but he was mighty relieved to see him emerging from the wood lower down with a Greek shepherd-boy in tow. Together they went down to the village. It proved to be Karoutes, about ten miles from where they were supposed to drop. Hamson lost no time in interrogating the villagers as to the whereabouts of the stores parachutes. They denied having ever seen them. Then Len spotted a small boy with a stick of plastic explosive. He chased him round the back of a house to find a number of youngsters being violently sick. 'The little perishers thought it was chocolate.' In spite of Hamson's command of Greek swearwords, it did them little good, and only a few paltry stores were produced. The container containing Len's personal kit was found, but not Hamson's.

Leaving Len sitting like an angry terrier on what stores they had gathered, Hamson went off with the shepherd to look for the Colonel and Barnes. He had no sooner gone than Barnes arrived with another shepherd. He and Myers had landed on the other side of the ravine but he had seen Len's chute in the morning and come across. Len's parachute was still caught up in the trees and the first priority was to retrieve the precious batteries; then they set off to join Myers. By mid-afternoon, tired, hungry and frustrated, the four of them were united. There was no sign of either of the other teams. 'A proper balls up,' was Len's private thought, but he kept his counsel.

Later a young Greek officer made an appearance, and the next morning led them cross country to a plateau where Myers set up his headquarters. Here they met their first *andarte* leader, apparently recommended to Myers by SOE Cairo.

> 'He was a bloody horrible little man, dressed in a filthy black uniform, no teeth, and covered in bandoliers and knives sticking out of his belt. The other five with him were little better.'

If these were the people with whom they were going to operate, Len did not think much of them. During the next two or three days there was considerable coming and going of Greeks. There was a surfeit of shouting, gesticulating, and frayed tempers as stores containers were reluctantly brought in, but 'not before the bastards had been through them and pinched most of the attractive items'.

Len had little idea of what was going on as nobody told him anything, but, when not scouring the hills for parachutes and their containers, he tried to get the wireless going. Opening the set he found a little notice saying *Insert Crystals here*; but there were no crystals; 'Of all bloody stupid things, Cairo had packed them in a stores container which had been lost, or someone had swiped them as diamonds.' To add to his fury the acid jars, badly packed, had smashed on landing, the charging engine was rusted solid, 'And the Colonel seemed to think that all he had to do was to pick up the handset to talk to Cairo'.

Behind enemy lines in the Falklands, in 1982, the SAS communicated as a matter of routine with their base in Hereford 8,000 miles away. 1942 was a far cry from today's highly-developed lightweight radio with its multifarious pre-set channels, built-in capture effect for faint signals, and communications satellites orbiting overhead. Nevertheless it is a fact of military life, even today, that signallers have the heaviest loads and, at the end of a day's march when others can rest, the signaller's real job begins.

In the days of unsophisticated HF radio, with its cumbersome ancillary equipment, there were a dozen or more jobs which were essential to good communications: the siting and erection of aerials, charging batteries, set maintenance, the time-consuming and exacting business of coding and decoding signals, to name a few. It is a truism that signallers tend to get pushed around, and more often than not they get the blame for failing to get through when the fault lies with the inadequacy of the equipment or impossible atmospheric or tactical conditions. It can be a lonely and thankless job.

On about the fourth day news reached Myers that a large Italian force was scouring the hills for them. Hastily hiding most of their recovered stores, they loaded essentials on to three mules and set off at dawn in pouring rain across the grain of the broken country. The first night was comparatively comfortable. Their Greek companions built rough brushwood shelters in the pine forest and one of them produced a live sheep which was quickly despatched for supper — the first meat Len had eaten since arriving in Greece.

Myers urgently needed to tell Cairo about their situation, and was becoming distinctly testy with Len. However, Len, professional signaller that he was, was already at work on the set and finally coaxed some life into it. He climbed up the mountain in the dark and pouring rain until he found a relatively flat piece of ground where he could erect his aerial. For two hours he tapped away, water pouring down his face and neck. He was soaked and numb. Cairo remained obstinately silent, but he was determined to keep trying, although he realized that without crystals he was attempting the miraculous. The crystals were on pre-set frequencies so it was near impossible to transmit which was what Myers desperately needed to do. It was still possible to receive by continuous fiddling and tuning to try by trial and error to pick up the correct frequency of the sender at the correct time.

Len tried again next morning without result, so the party moved off for a second exhausting day on the mountains. The weather, if anything, was worse and they were in the open, so they had to make do with improvised shelters made from parachutes. However, there were two pieces of good news; first a shepherd reported another party of Englishmen no more than two or three hours away; secondly, although they were yet to discover what good news he was, they acquired 'Baba Niko' (literally, Uncle Niko), a wizened old Greek who had spent a number of years in New York. Nevertheless, for Len it was:

'Up the ruddy mountain again, climb a tree to sling the aerial, and open up. I could hear Cairo this time — just — but with no crystals I couldn't get through. The Colonel didn't understand that — never did. And to make my day, when I got back to camp they had forgotten me so there was no food left.'

By that time the acidless batteries were flat, so it was pointless trying any more. However, next afternoon, 8 October, they found Woodhouse with his party on the plateau of Prophet Elias. His base was in a deep cave which was like a five-star hotel to the soaked, numb, bone-weary Len.

There was no respite for the signallers. Sergeant Mike Chitis, the wireless operator with Woodhouse, had not been able to get through to Cairo either. His set and his batteries had been badly damaged on landing, but his crystals had been found and his charging engine worked after a fashion. He and Len set to work to cannibalize one set in an effort to get the other to work. A pre-planned airdrop came in the following night which should have contained both food and wireless spares. It contained neither; only ammunition and boots — every one for the left foot.

Back from helping collect the drop on 10 October Len and Chitis climbed to a rocky escarpment high above the cave to spend hour after frustrating hour trying to raise Cairo. When they got down to the cave, again they found there was no food left for them. 'It was Baba Niko who went down to the village and came back with some bread, goat's cheese and a few olives. It was a feast to Mike and me.'

Their stay at Prophet Elias was to be short-lived. Rumours of another Italian force searching for them were brought up by the villagers and, after a frustrating couple of days, they were on their way again, once more in driving rain, to another cave that Baba Niko knew of near the village of Stromni. Larger and airier than the previous one, this was to be their home for many weeks.[8]

To get some shelter from the weather Len and Chitis established their wireless station in the ruins of a shepherd's hut on a rocky promontory nearby. There they resumed their efforts to get through to Cairo. But they had now run out of petrol for Chitis' charging engine so their batteries were flat. The Colonel was far from pleased. He seemed to think 'that we should be able to operate like Cable and Wireless'. That was unjust. Myers had found himself in a situation very different from the one painted in Cairo and needed urgently to tell them so.

It was Baba Niko who came to the rescue. He announced in his inimitable broken English with a strong Bronx accent, 'I duz know big machina in de water which give beeg fuck to batteries.' Whatever it was it was worth trying, so, strapping the batteries on to a donkey, Len and Baba Niko set off over yet another mountain. The machine proved to be a mill five or six hours march away with the millwheel driving a primitive electric plant. It did, however, charge the batteries. Len and Chitis redoubled their efforts to raise Cairo, crouched over their remaining set on their windy, freezing promontory. Within twenty-four hours their efforts were rewarded. It was one of those magic moments in a signaller's life when, from hundreds of miles away, however faintly or distorted by static, there came an answering morse signal from base.

Forty-five years later Woodhouse was to pay Len a well-deserved tribute:

'Len was a wonderfully determined young man, who never let anything get him down. In our first few weeks in Greece we had the greatest difficulty in establishing communications because our W/T sets were simply not up to the job, and anyway a lot of equipment was damaged

56

in the drop. But Len did in the end succeed in getting messages to Cairo in spite of the difficulties. In the circumstances of October, 1942, this was an almost incredible achievement, one of sheer pertinacity.'[9]

Few non-signals-trained officers really understand the wireless operator's difficulties and it is intensely frustrating when the wireless operators cannot get through and there is urgent traffic to be passed. In retrospect, Myers readily admits that he was impatient and frustrated by the lack of communications in the early days in Greece. It was understandable as it was not until 4 November that the first message was transmitted to Cairo.

Communications established, albeit tenuous and erratic, Len and Chitis worked night and day to pass long coded messages between Myers and Egypt. Coding and decoding was probably the most demanding aspect as the book code then in use, although simple, was laboriously time-consuming. One tiny error, or a morse letter misheard due to atmospherics, could render the message unintelligible.

The bringing down of the Gorgopotamus viaduct was one of the most dramatically successful guerrilla operations of the war. One hundred and fifty *andarte*, supported, advised and encouraged by twelve parachutists, cut the Germans' main line of communications in Greece for six weeks. Unfortunately it had not proved possible to do it in the short time-frame given to Myers. The viaduct fell on 26 November, about six weeks too late to have any effect on the outcome of the British breakout at Alamein, but still in time to prevent Rommel receiving reinforcements or supplies during his long retreat.

Operation HARLING had been conceived and born within a fortnight, and the Cairo planners wanted results within two weeks of that. In the event they were asking the impossible. Myers took with him a hotchpotch team who had never even met each other, let alone trained together, before arrival at Kabrit. The drop was postponed once, and on the second attempt only two out of the three aircraft dropped their teams. On the ground Myers was miles from the correct area, most of his stores were scattered and looted by the Greeks, and he did not join up with his second-in-command, Woodhouse, until 8 October. Then there was the frustrating and time-consuming business of making contact with the *andarte* leaders, as without their guides, local knowledge and firepower little could be achieved. Myers needed a secure base, he needed to make reconnaissances of the railway line, and he needed manpower for a strong attack if he was to destroy one of the three heavily-guarded viaducts.

While Len and Chitis were struggling to get one wireless into working order, and spending hour after endless hour tapping away in fruitless attempts to raise Cairo, planning and reconnaissances for an attack on the railway were going ahead.

Like most guerrilla forces, the *andarte*, and consequently Myers' group, depended for information and food on co-operative villagers. It was unsafe at this stage for the British to live in a village for any length of time. A suitable hide had to be found in the mountains within about an hour's climb of a village from which food and information could be carried up to the partisans. Initially Myers was in a cave on Mount Giona within striking distance of Karoutes; however, warning of an Italian search operation in the area compelled a move to a second, larger cave near the village of Stromni. They arrived there on 19 October only to be warned of yet more Italians in the vicinity. Baba Niko guided them safely away again to a well-concealed dell and cave but still within reach of Stromni.

At last Myers felt able to go and take a look at possible targets. All three viaducts were within fifteen miles of their new base. He chose to take Hamson, the Greek-speaking former commando officer, plus a local guide from Stromni called Yani Pistolis, who had come forward on the recommendation of Baba Niko. On 25 October they set off for the most southerly of the possible viaducts, Papadia.[10]

On high ground some 800 metres south-west of the bridge they settled into a position from which a good view was possible through binoculars. While Pistolis disappeared to contact a friend at the nearby railway station for details of the Italian guards, Myers studied the area. He was not enamoured with what he saw: too many Italians, too little cover, with well-sited guards posts on all likely approaches. When Pistolis returned at night to report about 200–300 Italians in the garrison, Myers mentally rejected Papadia as too risky. They would move on to Asopos that night.

The following day, from a vantage point 1,300 metres from the viaduct, Myers gazed through his glasses at the second possibility. The river which flowed under the bridge was at the bottom of a precipitous, narrow gorge with the mountains rising up a thousand feet or more on either side. A short way down the gorge, between Myers and the viaduct, was a high waterfall. There seemed no way a large party could approach to attack. The more he looked the more convinced he became that an assault was a high-risk venture. If he was to destroy it the operation was one for a small demolition party who would rely on stealth to place the charges. It was feasible but far from ideal. Hopefully the third possible objective — Gorgopotamos — would be more promising. It was.

This time Myers was able to get to an observation post only 300 metres from the bridge from which he had a reasonable view of the guards strolling about, although it was impossible to see their guardhouse or gauge their strength accurately; once more Pistolis volunteered to get this critical information from another friend who lived at the nearby railway junction of Lianokladi. The viaduct itself had masonry supports, which would be difficult to destroy, except for two. These two piers at the southern end were made of steel girders, comparatively easy to cut with the plastic explosive available. Myers had brought the photographs of the bridge and, after examining them and the bridge with great care, concluded that the four legs of each pier had L-shaped cross-sections. When Pistolis returned in an extremely agitated state just before dark to report that he had been stopped and questioned, they were forced to leave at once. The first leg led up the steep, slippery slopes of Mount Oiti, the forest-covered mountain west of the viaduct. The journey was exhausting, bitterly cold at night, and Pistolis got them lost at least once. In the early hours of 29 October the reconnaissance party arrived back at Stromni.

Myers decided, after some discussion, that, of the three, Gorgopotamos was the most suited to the sort of operation he had in mind. This was an attack by a strong force of *andarte*, first to overcome the guards at both ends of the viaduct, followed by the placing of the charges on the steel piers. Unfortunately he had no *andarte*. He had not made any contact with the Nationalist leader with whom he was supposed to co-operate — Colonel Zervas — who was reported some sixty miles away to the north-west, the other side of the mountains of central Greece. Neither had he yet made contact with Cairo.

On 2 November as, some 500 miles to the south, the 2nd New Zealand Division led the assault codenamed SUPERCHARGE to try to punch a hole in Rommel's line at Alamein, Woodhouse was despatched to find Zervas and bring him back with a strong force by 18 November. Unbeknown to the members of Operation HARLING, their efforts would be too late to influence the battle in the desert.

During the next two weeks of waiting several significant events occurred. The first was that Len and Chitis heard their first faint signal from Cairo and then, as related earlier, that exhilarating moment on 4 November of pure joy for the signallers when they were able to send their first message. It had taken five weeks, not through any fault of the operators but rather the result of a chain of circumstances, mainly technical, which had until then rendered their one set unable to transmit. Myers' reaction was: 'At last! Without delay I concocted for the twentieth time an up-to-date signal in order to ensure that the most important information would be got back to Cairo in our first message.'[11]

Also during this period Major Cook and his party from the third aircraft arrived at the cave. It transpired that on the second attempt Cook had refused to jump as there were still no recognizable fires on the ground. As the moon was not favourable for another month, it was 31 October before they tried again. Once more no ground signals, once more Cook was reluctant to jump until, as the Greek officer Captain Themie Marinos says, 'I gave him a boot up the arse.'[12] They had picked a bad spot. They landed in the Karpenisi valley where a sizable Italian garrison turned out in force to give them a hot reception. A vigorous fire-fight ensued with Cook's party scattering to play hide-and-seek with the Italians. All their containers were lost, including one that carried new plans of the viaducts. This was depressing news, as only a modicum of common sense would be sufficient to alert the enemy commander as to the partisans' likely targets. Fortunately the group was saved by the prompt and forceful intervention of a strong band of ELAS (Communist as distinct from Nationalist) *andarte* under Aris Veloukhiotis, a leader much feared for his ruthlessness. Cook and his group were rescued unscathed but lost their precious wireless. In the words of Len's old friend Doug Phillips, 'Cook panicked and abandoned the wireless station.'

On 18 November Woodhouse returned with the news that Zervas with some fifty men, together with Aris and another hundred, would arrive at Myers' headquarters the next day. Woodhouse had done a remarkable job, travelling a total distance of at least a hundred miles across the mountains, where the average day's journey was around ten miles. He had eventually found Zervas in the process of concluding a victorious skirmish with an Italian force that included artillery. Woodhouse was then in the area which the original plan for HARLING had directed him to be dropped. He was six weeks behind schedule.

Len remembers Woodhouse getting back in the middle of the night. He and Chitis had just got their heads down after about sixteen hours on the set when they were hauled out and given another long message. Wearily they set about coding it, then climbed to their hut to transmit it to Cairo. It was breakfast time by the time they had cleared it, 'If a few olives and goat's cheese can be called breakfast'.

One hundred and fifty *andarte* was more than enough for the attack; Myers was delighted. He took an immediate liking to Zervas who he described as having

'a short and rotund figure. When he laughed, as he often did, his whole body vibrated, and the merry sparkle in his eyes belied the black, hairy fierceness of a heavily bearded face. . . . He wore an old army officer's khaki tunic devoid of all insignia, khaki riding-breeches and a pair of brown, rather over-large riding-boots. An unpolished Sam Browne belt around his ample waist supported a small automatic pistol and a jewelled dagger whose sheath was liable to stick out from his stomach at a jaunty angle when he sat down.'[13]

Zervas readily agreed Myers' outline plan but said they should move to the village of Mavrolithari where everyone could be billeted in houses — a previously unheard-of luxury. On 20 October, aided by a train of twenty mules, the entire band moved to the new location. Snow had fallen that night, covering the forest and mountain sides with a beautiful blanket of whiteness.

It was at Mavrolithari that Aris joined forces with Zervas and Myers. It was to be the only time during the war that Communists and Nationalists fought successfully alongside each other. Even on this occasion Aris was disobeying his superiors in Athens. Again Myers has given a vivid pen picture of the ELAS leader.

'He was a small man, of the same height as Zervas, but of a more wiry build. His long black beard, which balanced his Cossack cap of black fur, could make his face look benign and almost monk-like. But his eyes were deep-set and, except when he smiled, there was much hardness in his features. Only when mellowed by alcohol did he ever relax. Silent, and inclined to be dour, he always gave me the impression of being on guard against someone or something.'[14]

Aris was to show his savage streak while at Mavrolithari. One of his *andarte* had been caught stealing. Aris was called to meet out summary justice. The wretched man was stripped naked and thrashed by one of Aris' young recruits, then Aris pulled out his pistol and calmly shot him through the head.

Wireless traffic doubled with *andarte* demands for weapons, equipment and explosives, but, apart from what they read in Myers' signals, the three sergeants knew nothing of his plans. It was then that Len's lasting affection for New Zealanders was born. 'Tom Barnes and Arthur Edmonds were the only officers who spoke to the sergeants and told us a bit of what was going on.' Barnes was to be in charge of the main demolition party at the viaduct and Len, with his self-taught knowledge of explosives, used to give him a hand in preparing the charges when wireless duties permitted. He asked, also, to be one of Barnes' party on the viaduct, and Barnes readily agreed.

Considerable time was spent warming the plastic explosives by hand, and pressing the sticks into wooden L-shaped moulds so that no time would be wasted placing it around the girders of the viaduct.

Myers' plan was agreed by both *andarte* leaders. The force available was divided into seven groups each with a separate task. First in the order of march, because they had the furthest to go, was Cook with fifteen ELAS *andarte*, their task being to cut the railway line about a mile south of the viaduct and prevent any reinforcements from interfering with the main attack. On arrival Cook was to cut the telephone lines, but not the railway track, unless enemy approached or he saw the green Very light flare go up indicating the final withdrawal.

Next came another party of ELAS men under Marinos whose task and orders were identical to Cook's but who were taking up position a mile to the north of the viaduct. This was thought to be the most likely direction of approach by Italians reacting from Lamia, only six miles away. Myers anticipated that perhaps two hours after firing started the enemy reinforcements could be nearing the scene.

Behind Marinos came Captain Michalli, Zervas' Adjutant, in command of a mixed Communist and Nationalist group of forty men. His was thought to be the most difficult part of the operation apart from the actual demolition. He was to secure the southern end of the viaduct where the Italians had their greatest strength. The steel piers that were to be blown were at this end, so it was essential to subdue all resistance in this area before the demolition party went to work. For these reasons Michalli's group was the largest. Once he had taken the area he was to fire a white Very light.

The fourth group in the long column consisted of Zervas' men, about thirty strong, whose objective was the north end of the viaduct. As in the south its task was the destruction of the defenders in the area.

Following behind this party was Myers, with his joint headquarters which included Woodhouse, Zervas and Aris. Myers' intention was to cross the river by a narrow plank bridge some distance upstream from the viaduct before moving along the southern bank to a position from which he could watch progress, particularly of the assault on the crucial southern end. Behind him would be the reserve force of thirty men under Zervas' second-in-command, Komninas. This group would be controlled by Myers and only committed on his orders. At the rear came Barnes, his demolition party (which included Len) with eight mules carrying some 400 pounds of explosive all moulded into the required shape.

As with all military plans, timing was critical. How long would it take to march from Mavrolithari to the forward concentration point, a group of huts in the dense forest on the slopes of Mount Oiti? How long would it take to get from the huts to the viaduct and get everybody into position? How long would it take the assault parties to secure their objectives? How long would it take the demolition party to bring down the two piers? How long would it be before enemy reinforcements arrived?

The intention was to attack during the night of 25/26 November. The initial march to the huts could be done in daylight during the day with the final approach being made from the forward rendezvous after dark. Allowing about six hours for this phase everybody should be in position by 10 p.m. Zervas was keen to make this the H-Hour, but Myers and Aris felt another hour would be wise. At 11 p.m. the assault would start simultaneously at both ends of the viaduct. It was estimated that two hours would be needed for the preparation of each of the piers for destruction by Barnes' party. Enemy reaction from Lamia could be expected in two, so there was every possibility of a prolonged fight for time to protect the group blowing the bridge.

On 23 November Zervas and Aris, who had not seen the ground at all, insisted they carry out a final personal reconnaissance, so Myers and Woodhouse took them on, with a small escort, ahead of the main body. A thick mist and clouds, however, prevented any observation at dawn on 24 November so it was not until the morning of the 25th that a cold, somewhat weary group of officers crawled forward to view their target. Myers said later, 'We got some excellent glimpses of the viaduct. Several hundred feet below us it looked like a toy bridge.'[15] After an hour Aris and Zervas were satisfied, so the group withdrew up Mount Oiti to a pre-arranged rendezvous just inside the forest at a disused sawmill. At 4 p.m. the main body began arriving. The striking force had assembled within a mile of the viaduct and several thousand feet above it.

For Len the approach march was exhilarating; the endless hours on the set, the indifferent food over the past weeks were forgotten as at long last he was going to see some real action. He had the utmost confidence in Barnes; 'He was one of those blokes you trust with your life without a second thought.'

As Len neared the viaduct the roar of the water in the gorge below drowned the noise of boots and mules slipping on patches of bare rock. The demolition party made a cautious approach. Two or three hundred yards from the viaduct they halted and looked up. Framed against the night sky the awe-inspiring spans of the Gorgopotamos viaduct stood out majestically against the moonlit sky. Len felt almost sorry that something so beautiful had to be destroyed. His thoughts were abruptly interrupted when he was called forward to the headquarters group.

'Myers seemed worried, and there was a lot of shouted whispering going on above the noise of the water. He told me to take the wireless and get back to the sawmill, call Cairo and keep them on listening watch, report the success signal as soon as I saw it, and stand by with the set open till he got back. If it went wrong I was to report what I could, then scarper and make my own way back to Mavrolithari.'

Len was furious, although he could not show it in front of Myers, and Myers was not about to use precious time explaining what had happened to his sergeant wireless operator whose place was not really with the demolition party.

Back up at the sawmill Len set up his aerial and called Cairo:

'I got them after a few tries but the signals were weak because we were the wrong side of the mountain. I told them to stand by, then I coded up a couple of alternative messages. For once I didn't get my head down.'

It was a long, lonely vigil waiting on the top of the mountain virtually on his own. He had little Greek at that stage, so the two *andarte* escorts were poor company. Len knew from Barnes that H-Hour for the attack was 11 p.m. Eleven o'clock came and went, and the minutes ticked by with agonizing slowness. As a precaution Len re-checked the coding of his failure message. Still the minutes dragged by until at about 11.20 p.m. all hell was let loose at both ends of the viaduct. The staccato hammering of automatic weapons filled the night. 'Christ, I thought, what the hell have they run into?'

Len tried to visualize what was going on as the firing rose to a crescendo, then died down, only to be renewed with increasing intensity from a different direction. After what seemed an aeon of time (the battle lasted over an hour before the ends of the viaduct were secured and the demolition party could go in), Len saw a white Very light curve into the air. But there was still no explosion. He remembers saying out loud, over and over again, 'Come on, Barnsey, come on,' while cursing Myers for leaving him out.

Then the whole sky lit up. A second or two later a great roar of sound rolled up the valley, shaking the sawmill even at that distance. Len tore up the failure message and got on the set. 'Of all bloody things it chose that moment to go U/S.'

Len's disappointment at not being in at the kill had been brought about by the first hitch of the operation. As Myers led the headquarters towards the plank bridge to cross to the south side of the river, Aris and Zervas held back. They had no wish to cross over. They felt that the higher ground on the north bank would give them a better view and ability to control events. Myers wanted the headquarters, reserve and demolition party over near the most critical end of the viaduct. There was an impasse. The loud whispering that Len heard was the tail-end of the argument. Neither of the two *andarte* leaders would budge, so, with great reluctance, Barnes was told to cross on his own, and watch for Myers to flash his torch as a signal that he should proceed with the demolition.[16]

Eleven o'clock came and went. Then, just as Myers felt something must surely have gone wrong, pandemonium broke out at the north end of the bridge. Zervas' unit opened up with stens, rifles and two machine guns. The

Italian response was equally noisy, with at least three machine guns blazing away from their bunkers. This fire-fight continued for some twenty minutes before dying down slightly. Zervas expressed concern that at that rate ammunition would soon run out. Then heavy firing broke out in the south. At last Michalli's men were in action; indeed, his shouts of encouragement could be heard, then cheers as the Italians seemed to be getting the worst of it.

It was the northern end that was causing anxiety. The decision was taken to put in the reserve force under Komninos. By a strange quirk of fate having the headquarters and reserve on the north bank was to prove fortuitous after all. Komninos was able to reinforce the attack quickly. More brisk firing ensued. After another twenty minutes, however, no real progress had been made. The enemy continued to resist. Zervas claimed he had been betrayed, that the Italians had been forewarned. He said that he would fire the green Very light — the withdrawal signal — in another ten minutes if the bridge was not captured by then. He demanded the pistol. It could not be found. Inadvertently Komninos had taken it forward with him. Myers sent Woodhouse to retrieve it, with strict orders to keep it himself and on no account to fire it without his instructions.[17]

The situation was now critical, with the issue in the balance. Neither end of the bridge had been secured after nearly an hour's battle; ammunition would not last much longer at that rate of firing; the reserve had been committed; the demolition party could not be deployed and Zervas was advocating a retreat. Then, just as Myers was beginning to feel desperate, a crescendo of firing, cheers, and the firing of a white light at the southern end announced that Michalli had secured his objective.

Myers made an immediate decision. He dashed down to the edge of the gorge opposite where Barnes was lying up, flashed his torch and yelled, 'Go in, Tom! The south end of the bridge is in our hands. Go in! I will join you as soon as possible.' Barnes acknowledged.

After another wait of perhaps a quarter of an hour Myers again went forward, this time to try to sort out what was happening at the northern end. He failed to find Komninos, but gained the impression that resistance was crumbling. Finally the shrill blast of a whistle told him that the demolition on the first pier was ready for firing. Everybody cowered down. Thirty seconds, one minute, two minutes later the brilliant flash, followed by a gigantic bang that was heard in Lamia as two of the steel spans heaved up and collapsed with a roar of rending metal and twisted girders. This dramatic success galvanized the *andarte* in the north for a final push which routed the few remaining enemy. The viaduct had been blown and both ends captured.

Myers went out along the bridge to inspect the damage. He yelled down at Barnes, trying unsuccessfully to be heard above the rushing river. At last

Hamson answered. Another forty minutes were needed to bring down a second pier and cut the two spans lying partially in the water. There was great urgency as at about this time heavy firing and explosions were heard a mile or so to the north. Italian reinforcements had arrived.

In fact it did not take forty minutes. With Zervas now insisting the withdrawal flare be fired, Myers had to shout across to Woodhouse that on no account should it be fired until the second explosion. Within twenty minutes it came. Another flash, another huge crash, the fallen spans heaved again, but no additional span fell. Within seconds the green light sailed gracefully over the scene of destruction. The withdrawal began. The entire operation had been a remarkable success, at the cost of only one *andarte* lightly wounded.

When Myers reached the sawmill it was nearly dawn. All Len remembers him saying was, 'Why the hell aren't you through to Cairo?' and 'Get the wireless packed up and get cracking'. In the aftermath of the night's tensions Myers was understandably brusque, but Len 'realized the man was absolutely knackered, so I just said, "Well done Sir", and got packed up.'

There was great rejoicing at Mavrolithari when they got back on 27 November, but Len felt distinctly out of it and disinclined to join in the festivities.

'I was about the only bloke who hadn't got a war story to tell, but I knew by then that I was staying behind with Monty Woodhouse when the rest of HARLING went out, so I reckoned there would be other opportunities.'

CHAPTER FIVE

OPERATION ANIMALS

'Len always was a randy little bastard, and here he was behind enemy lines knocking off the Greek officers' laundress. He was never short of a clean shirt.' Bill Weatherley, former Catterick contemporary of Len.[1]

The authorities were to be generous with awards for the Gorgopotamos success. Within three months Myers received notification that he and Woodhouse had been given the DSO; Barnes, Edmonds, Hamson and Captain Michalli (Zervas' Adjutant) the MC; Zervas and Aris the OBE, (although the latter's subsequent anti-British activities led to his award being cancelled) and Baba Niko the MBE. Captain Barnes had been recommended for the DSO for his great coolness at the viaduct, where he had had to remould all the plastic explosives under fire. The problem was that all the girders were U-shaped rather than L-shaped, so all the work of preparation of the charges was wasted.

Unbeknown to Len, Myers had also recommended him for the BEM for his unflagging efforts on the radio under such adverse conditions for so long.[2] Despite the fact that to Len he seemed not to appreciate the operator's problems, this was not so. As Myers' headquarters operator, Len's duties were particularly arduous and stressful as there was an even greater urgency for his set to be functioning and, once it was, the workload was intense. As Myers was later to write in his matter-of-fact way:

'It took Len, and the other operators whom I put under his charge, a month to get either wireless to work. Len was easily the most cheerful of the three operators. . . . He was always uncomplaining about the hardships he had to endure from time to time.'[3]

Len's father was to cherish two flimsy wartime letter-cards, found much-fingered in his everyday jacket after his death, from HQ Force 133 (cover for SOE Cairo).[4] Ironically the first to arrive told him of his son's second decoration, the immediate award of the MM, the citation for which appears in Appendix 5.

If there were deservedly generous rewards for some after the destruction of the viaduct, there was undeserved retribution for others. The Germans selected thirteen innocent civilians from Lamia to be shot in reprisal. This unfortunate group was taken to Gorgopotamos to be executed on the spot. A memorial to their memory was erected after the war and remains to this day. Sadly, also, Costa Pistolis, the brother of Myers' guide, the schoolteacher who gave such valuable information on the Italian defences, was arrested, interrogated and later shot. It is of some comfort to know that after the war the British authorities were able to assist his widow and two children.[5]

Operation HARLING had been planned as a quick strike at the German railway communications in Greece with a view to disrupting the flow of supplies to North Africa. With a few exceptions, the personnel who had parachuted in had volunteered to do so on the understanding that they would be pulled out afterwards. With the viaduct down at the end of November, Myers and most of his team anticipated being back in Cairo for Christmas. It was not to be.

Major Woodhouse, Captain Marinos and two signallers, Sergeants Willmott and Phillips, were the stay-behind party. Myers was to lead the remainder across the mountains to the north-west to a beach rendezvous just south of Parga, from where a submarine was scheduled to evacuate them.

For Len the immediate priority was to get his set working again. He racked his brain to remember what he had seen at Catterick when they were building the Singapore transmitter. They had a cottage at the bottom of the village, but it was so cold that 'our fingers were all thumbs'. They could only work on the set for a few minutes before having to stop to thaw their frozen hands. Food was desperately short and, busy on the set, they had little time to scavenge for themselves.

On 17 December, on one of their rare contacts with Cairo, Len took down a long, coded signal. It was corrupt and they could not check it back as Cairo had gone off the air again. Len, by sheer persistence, managed to unscramble enough of it to indicate that a stores drop was scheduled for two nights hence. 'Woodhouse was pleased with this, and I think he was beginning to realize that the wireless difficulties were not all the fault of the signallers.'

All four of the stay-behind party hoped fervently that the drop would include a new wireless, requested many weeks before. Two nights later, on 19 December, 1942, not only did a new wireless station arrive but so, unheralded, did Captain Bill Jordan, Royal New Zealand Signals. 'He was the best Christmas present possible.'

Len and Phillips had gone up to the headquarters house in the village to grab any wireless equipment before anyone else got to it, and there was the new officer. His shirt was off and a Greek doctor was slapping bits of sticking plaster on his ribs. It was obvious to Len that the newcomer was in considerable pain, but he shook their hands, promising he would be down to see them later.[6]

Jordan had been sent in as a professional signals officer to sort out the HARLING communication difficulties. He had landed wide of the dropping zone, his parachute had collapsed swinging him into a boulder breaking six ribs, dislocating his elbow and damaging his kidneys. Because of the corrupt signal from Cairo, Marinos had been surprised to find him among the stores parachutes. After a cold and painful night in the open, Marinos hoisted Jordan on to a mule before setting off over a mountain to the village of Megalohari, where Woodhouse had his headquarters with Zervas. The nine-hour journey in snow, on slippery mountain tracks, had been agony and, on one occasion, the mule's saddle strap had broken, throwing Jordan to the ground.

After a meal, and despite his injuries, Jordan went down to the wireless operator's cottage at the foot of the village — sergeants did not eat with officers — to introduce himself properly. He has described his first meeting with them:

'Len had the most to say. He was a perky, fresh-faced, highly intelligent youngster who had been in the Army since boy service. He inquired if I was satisfied with the manner in which my ribs had been bandaged. I said it was rather unusual and asked if he knew how to do it. "Of course I do," said Len, with plain contempt for anyone so dumb as not to know how to strap up broken ribs. . . . I knew I had found a useful lad. Len, I felt, was one on whom I could rely in a crisis.'[7]

It was Len who gave Jordan an articulate and professional summary of the backlog of wireless problems.

'Many of the stores dropped have been lost because of inaccurate dropping and the depredations of the Greek guerrillas or villagers who found the containers. Jars of acid were smashed because they had not been properly packed. One complete drop went straight into the hands of the Italians. Another was grabbed in a village which the Italians attacked. They got a complete wireless station when they left. Now we have one wireless set, two batteries (both flat), no acid, and two charging engines, one of which was rusted solid on arrival and the other fell down a ravine strapped to a mule. The mule survived but the charging engine did not. It is at another village some four hours away where there is a man who said he was a mechanic and could repair it.'[8]

The next morning the rest of Jordan's wireless kit was brought in by the guerrillas. The batteries were serviceable, but the charging engine had not been properly packed and had smashed on impact. Worse still, it was rusted up and would have been useless even if intact. It had obviously not been inspected for a long time.

Jordan then spotted two more figures approaching, one of whom was staggering under an enormous load. Len explained that it was their charging engine being returned after repair. Jordan remembers the incident well:

'I saw a frail, emaciated woman carrying on her back a Charhorse charging engine. It was the heaviest engine dropped on such operations, with a cast-iron casing. When the woman collapsed against a rise in the ground someone cut the ropes which strapped the engine to her back. A man could lift the engine only with difficulty. The woman lay back, panting like an exhausted animal.'[9]

Len had never seen a man so angry. When the husband, who was quite unable to understand what all the fuss was about, had the gall to explain to Jordan that the woman was carrying it 'because it was too heavy for the mule', Jordan exploded. His language, in both Greek and English, possibly with a bit of Maori thrown in, put his previous outburst in the shade. 'I thought he would murder the man with his bare hands, or, worse, do himself lasting damage from sheer fury.' Len suggested mildly that he would get used to the ways of the mountains, only to find himself on the receiving end of 'a tongue-lashing I'll never forget'. No such thing was going to happen while Jordan was around. He made it abundantly clear to Len and Phillips that if there were no mules they would carry the engine themselves. 'It showed us what sort of bloke Jordan was, and we liked what we saw.'

Jordan's temper was not improved when they tested the repaired charging engine and found it started but produced no charge, never a surprise in the Greek mountains where self-professed experts on almost any subject could be found. Nevertheless, Jordan was determined to try to get through to Cairo that night with his own batteries while they were still fully charged. Len opened up the set at the scheduled time and tapped out their callsign. Weak but readable came Cairo's answering morse. Len looked up with a grin. Jordan silently grasped his hand.

Myers and his party had had a terrible Christmas. With Captain Michalli and twelve *andarte* as their guide and escort they had to make a ten-day journey across the mountains to the coast in mid-winter. Myers had sent a message via a courier to the partisan leader in Athens to radio Cairo for the evacuation to be on the west coast, about five miles south of Parga sometime between 22 and 25 December. The miserable weather, insufficient food and the gruelling march with little sleep steadily eroded their strength. By the time they reached the rendezvous area all were in a wretched condition, only buoyed up by the thought of the submarine. As Myers was well aware, there was no guarantee it would be there; he had no wireless contact with Cairo, so could not know the response to his evacuation message.

The first night they took it in turns to keep flashing the prearranged recognition signal. Nothing. The next day they hid and tried again on the second night. Again nothing. It was now Christmas Eve. Myers has said of that time, 'It was the first time I had experienced continuous hunger, and the feelings of insecurity and depression which accompany it. . . . We were rather a dejected group.' That night was a repeat of the first two — fruitless flashing of torches in the biting cold. Christmas day saw a thoroughly disheartened group. Just as they were preparing to start the final night of signalling a courier arrived with a message in Woodhouse's handwriting. It confirmed their fears.

A new wireless set had been received together with a message that no submarine was coming. No explanation; just the fact that a Captain Bill Jordan would be dropped in two days with fresh written orders for Myers. Myers confesses, 'I was by now too weak and tired to succeed in instilling a measure of humour into this group of bitterly disappointed volunteers. . . . The memory of our journey back from the coast is still like that of a nightmare.'[10] They arrived at Megalohari on 9 January, 1943.

Myers spent a long time thinking through the implications of the long message Jordan had brought. It started with the good news: confirmation of the various decorations awarded for the rushing river operation. Then came the bombshell. Myers was promoted brigadier with the task of organizing, equipping and training guerrillas throughout Greece. This was to lead to full-scale partisan operations in the field against enemy lines of communications. The aim — to make the Germans believe an Allied assault on the mainland of Greece was imminent — so that manpower and resources were tied down, and thus unable to reinforce Sicily or Southern Italy, where an invasion would eventually take place. SOE's plan envisaged supplying the whole of Greece with arms, ammunition and explosives. Starting in March with eight sorties, the logistics would build up to twenty-four sorties monthly from June onwards until the winter restricted flying activities.

Myers was required to submit a plan to Cairo. His first step was to gather all his team to explain the new circumstances. He told them it was now vital for them all to remain in Greece. There was a major task ahead that could have enormous consequences for the war effort. He had to be careful, however; if the maximum enthusiasm was to be maintained, only a select few of his senior officers must know that the role of the *andarte* was diversionary.[11] Len, and the other operators who handled the messages would know, but most personnel and all the *andarte* must believe that their efforts were designed to prepare for Allied landings in Greece. Only then could they be relied upon to give of their best.

The plan that emerged was to divide the country into four regions, each under a lieutenant-colonel. The officers concerned would be Tom Barnes at Epirus, Arthur Edmonds in Roumeli, Rufus Sheppard in Olympus and Nick Hammond in Macedonia. Myers suggested that, if the Peloponnese was to be included, then Denys Hamson should take charge there. Cook was to be sent to contact the partisans in Albania.[12]

With the new wireless set and the huge potential expansion of operations, Len's life, for day after day, night after night, week after week, revolved around swapping ever longer messages with Cairo.

The volume of signal traffic increased tenfold. The signals team, Jordan, Len, Phillips, and for a short time before HARLING dispersed, Chitis, set to encoding, decoding, transmitting and receiving often faint and garbled signals, charging batteries, maintaining and repairing equipment — all the hundred and one tasks that fall to wireless operators in the field. Above all, there was hour after hour of painstaking checking and re-checking the signals, trying to make sense of the inevitable corrupt passages, and breaking down Myers' long complicated messages, including his War Diary from the time HARLING had dropped, into manageable lengths for transmission. All this was done under primitive conditions, in bitter cold when frozen fingers could hardly hold a pencil.

Jordan had not met Myers before, and found him 'unaffable'.[13] But he quickly agreed to his request that nobody other than the signals team should enter the signals cottage now that so much highly classified traffic was being handled. This pleased Len, particularly as he had been unable to keep Greek *andarte* officers from coming and going at will, leaning over his shoulder and reading what he was doing. Now even Myers knocked before he came in.

Jordan regarded the four months (January-May, 1943) that followed as the hardest of his life:

'We worked sixteen to eighteen hours a day, usually with only a handful of dried beans and a little corn bread to eat each day. Sometimes we were lucky enough to get a little goat's meat. Lack of food in the depths of winter, with poor working conditions and insufficient warmth, inevitably undermined our health.'[14]

Jordan drove the signallers hard; he drove himself harder, and Len marvelled at the stamina of the man. 'He must have been in hellish pain the first few weeks from his injuries on landing, and I knew he was peeing blood, even if he wouldn't admit it.' Jordan was the sort of officer he understood, and to whom he could give his unqualified loyalty: 'Another Tom Barnes in a way, but he was a pro in my own corps, and a better wireless operator that I was.'

Within a day or so of arriving, Jordan had moved into the signallers' cottage rather than staying with the headquarters officers in the doctor's house. Shortly after this he decided that, in the circumstances, the signals group would be on first-name terms with each other. Nevertheless, there was never any question as to who was 'boss'. His discipline, if different, was as strict as any Len had known: 'He even stopped me smoking on the set.'

Jordan had his own views on officer-men relationships, views that were to influence Len strongly:

'Relations between officers and other ranks were, I knew, not as free or as intelligent in mutual understanding as in the Australian and New Zealand Armies. There was nothing wrong with the discipline. Allowing for the usual exceptions, cordial relations existed between officers and men. More may be asked of an officer to maintain discipline under such circumstances, but on my reckoning the end result was something far healthier than the attitudes which existed in the British Army at the time. . . . British soldiers often regarded a friendly attitude on the part of an officer with suspicion.'[15]

Today the SAS practice of calling their soldiers by their Christian names, and the soldiers calling their officers 'boss', is still widely misunderstood. It is not a practice that will work in more conventional units, but in the SAS there are practical reasons for it, and it is a privilege that has to be earned on both sides. This was Jordan's conclusion, deep behind enemy lines.

Jordan quickly created a happy, close-knit small team which was reflected in the remarkable results they achieved. Communications with Cairo were now working well, but atmospheric conditions on the frequencies they were using meant that all signals traffic had to be sent and received at night. In daylight the signallers had all their other multifarious tasks to do and, for sheer survival, forage for food and fuel. This was not part of their job. Provision of these basics was the responsibility of Zervas' *andarte*. Jordan would make frequent and forceful complaints, whereupon food would improve for a day or two, then revert to normal. Fuel was desperately short. The andarte would not lift a finger to help: 'Just sat on their arses all day smoking and talking politics'.

According to Jordan, it was Len who solved the fuel crisis by taking down the fences round their houses. 'Oh yes, they protested all right, but Jordan threatened to burn their furniture as well. We got plenty of fuel after that.'

It was several weeks before Jordan realized that Len had another source of warmth, although he had been suspicious at the frequency with which Len used his few off-duty hours to disappear to see about his *dhobi*. When Bill Weatherley (another former Catterick boy soldier) arrived as a reinforcement, he was quick to spot what was going on.

'Len always was a randy little bastard, and here he was behind enemy lines knocking off the Greek officers' laundress. He was never short of a clean shirt'.[16]

Len's response: 'Well, they say it is the best way to learn a language, and I spoke good Greek by the time I came out.'

Concurrently, another woman began to play a less warming part in their lives, although she generated considerable heat in the signals team. Cairo changed frequency to a better one, but from Myers' headquarters they picked up a powerful Soviet transmitter operating on a frequency close to that of Cairo. 'I'd just finish fine-tuning to Cairo to give them the go-ahead to transmit when this bloody woman would come booming through, blotting out everything.' Jordan transmitted in every language he knew, and he spoke several, to get her off the air — none of it polite.

Moves were by then second nature to Len, but he found it irritating that no sooner had they got effective communications going with Cairo than reports of an Italian column approaching caused a move for several days. Packing and unpacking a wireless station is a time-consuming business given the type of equipment they had. They had no sooner settled back into Megalochori when they got word from Myers to move to Skolikaria — which just happened to be the other side of a mountain range. It was still midwinter with deep snow on the precipitous and narrow mountain tracks — as the crow flew a distance of about eight miles — in time over ten hours. It became an exhausting journey for the already weakened signals team as they fought to keep the mules with their previous wireless station from falling down the side of the mountain.

It was at Skolikaria that Jordan and Len narrowly escaped capture. There had been an alert during the night, but Jordan decided to complete the wireless schedule to Cairo, by which time the panic seemed to have died down, as so many of them did. In the morning they saw the rest of the team loading mules in preparation for moving off, so they started to pack up the wireless station. Just then, in Jordan's words:

'a frantic woman rushed in screaming, "The Italians, the Italians! They are already in the village. Run . . . ooooh it's too late".'[17]

Len has some strong views about this particular move, and it turned out to be a near thing.

'The rest of the party had pushed off with the *andarte* without telling us they were going, the bastards. There were no mules left. Bill (Jordan) literally chucked a villager's load off his mule — a terrible thing to do, I suppose, but we had to save the wireless station as it was our only link with Cairo.'

Driving the little mule unmercifully, they escaped out of the top end of the village as the Italians came in at the bottom, leaving much of their personal kit behind. Jordan remarked that he hated the thought of the Italians getting all their personal gear, to which Len responded, 'The Eyties will have to be quick to beat the Greeks to it'. Len's quick humour did not affect his great sadness at seeing the village of Skolikaria going up in flames.

Jordan was later to compliment Len on his part in this incident:

'Amid my gloomy thoughts of what had taken place — a gloom that was deepened by hunger and cold and the hazards of the snow-covered mountains — I had the consolation of knowing that the link with Cairo was preserved. Its retention was due in no small measure to the loyalty and reliability of Len.'[18]

Settled first in the village of Mesopyrgo, then further south in Avlaki, wireless communications suddenly improved dramatically with a new and much more powerful transmitter coming on stream in Cairo. It did nothing to alleviate the burden on the signallers. Brigadier Myers had fallen seriously ill in the late January of 1943 and hovered near death for several weeks. To the backlog of wireless traffic to be cleared was added urgent requests for drugs and medical advice. It was indicative of the volume of traffic that when Myers returned to the helm six weeks later they had only just cleared the last of his war diary and other low priority signals.

Their relief and sense of achievement was reflected in Len's renewed interest in his *dhobi* — the laundress travelled with the headquarters — but it was shortlived. 'Cairo hit us between the eyes with a lengthy directive that occupied several days of wireless transmission. It was followed by nights of intense cipher work.' The directive confirmed plans for Operation ANI-MALS, requiring Myers to organize widespread sabotage throughout Greece as a diversion to the planned Allied landings in Sicily. The ensuing wireless traffic added yet another dimension to the overworked signals team.

In early April, 1943, the living conditions were transformed by the arrival of Captain Ross Bower as personal assistant to Myers who was to take charge of administration. Bower, a former guardsman, had parachuted in, to Len's astonishment, wearing polished boots and burnished brass badges of rank on his shoulders. 'About the only thing missing was a bearskin and a sword.' To Jordan, Bower's arrival in Greece meant 'a radical change in our whole way of living . . . Food was put on a proper basis and bought in the plains. Crockery and cutlery were purchased. . . . There was a general smartening up.'[19] To Len Bowers was good news but, being an old soldier, he kept well out of his way, 'in case I got my name taken for a haircut'.

Four reinforcement signallers arrived at about this time to ease the load. They were a help but, in Len's view, 'only some'.

'One seemed to think he'd come to a Butlin's Holiday Camp — complained about everything and was useless. Bill sent him off somewhere a lot less comfortable — to the SOE team with the communists. Another had a terrible stutter and even stuttered on the morse key, so he wasn't much better. The other two had much to learn, but they did so in time.'

The intricacies of Greek politics between rival groups, the intransigence and sheer bloody-mindedness of Aris and his communists, and the extraordinary patience and diplomacy displayed by Myers and Woodhouse, are not part of Len's story, except insofar as they affected the wireless traffic and the demands on the signals team. Len was critical of the volume of wireless traffic — 'Thought we were bloody Cable & Wireless' — but later appreciated that the issues were a great deal more complicated than he thought when he damned the eyes of the headquarters for yet another message to be encoded. But the strain was beginning to tell. Jordan and Len had a serious confrontation. Jordan recalls:

'I don't think it was about anything important. What I do remember is that the basic cause was exhaustion from overwork; we were both overtired and undernourished. Len had been in the country longer than I had and he had had no let up, particularly since I had arrived.'[20]

As the junior, it was Len who was wheeled up in front of Woodhouse. There was no punishment as such, rather that Len should have a rest from the strain. He was sent off on what would today be called Local R and R (rest and recuperation). In Greece in the circumstances of the time that meant

8. Len commissioned into the
General Service Corps, September,
1944.

9. Operation ALOES (see p.88).
Centre, the "legendary Colonel Passy,
chief of De Gaulle's Secret Service"
(p.89). On the right is the girl Len
was asked to marry.

10. "We saw this Bentley parked behind a German headquarters, so we borrowed it" (p.93).

11. "Captain Jacob Staal was a thirty-one-year-old Dutch-born South African attached to the Queen's Own Dorset Yeomanry, seconded to SOE" (p.94).

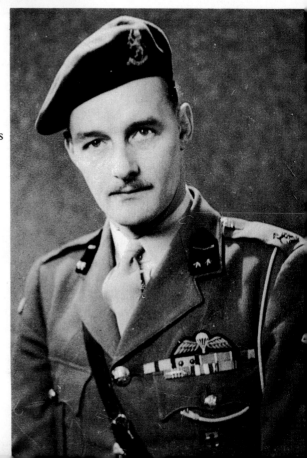

being billeted on his own in a Greek house in a different village, in this case Trinklinos. As Len says, 'It sounds crazy, behind the lines in the middle of a war. It turned out quite a leave.'

The Greek family were more than hospitable, and Len remembers their many kindnesses with gratitude, not least sleeping between sheets for the first time in many months, and his hostess's cooking. His days were spent lying in the sun in the family olive grove, reading whatever he could get his hands on (he had become an avid reader of every book included in their air drops). The evenings were equally enjoyable, drinking and gossiping in the taverna, with the added attraction of chatting to the local girls — he now spoke passable colloquial Greek.

By the time Len reported back from his leave HARLING team members had been dispersed to the various regions set up by Myers in his plan to coordinate the countrywide sabotage envisaged in ANIMALS. Captain Jordan was given an area of his own, complete with a band of *andarte*. He asked Myers if he could take Len as his signaller, but this was turned down as, according to Myers, he could not be spared.

Len's old friend from Catterick, Doug Phillips, was no longer at the headquarters and Len felt his absence keenly. He was never to see Phillips again as, tragically, he was later to be blown up by a mine laid by ELAS.

The headquarters moved to Theodhoriana, and Myers was away for much of the time. Len was left to his own devices but was pleased that Barnes, the New Zealand sapper, was still based with him. Additionally, a Warrant Officer, Stan Smith, had arrived to take charge of the headquarters wireless team. In due course Myers moved his headquarters elsewhere to position himself roughly on the boundary between the rival EDES (Zervas) and ELAS forces. The situation was a delicate and unpleasant one in which the communists had already launched a number of unprovoked attacks on Zervas' *andarte*.

While in Theodhoriana the village of Voulgareli, across the valley, was bombed by a mixture of German Stukas and Italian Savona divebombers. 'Obviously it was meant for us, but they had got the HQ village wrong.' Len had a grandstand view. As one Stuka pulled out of its dive, a Savona coming in from the other direction hit it. The Stuka stalled, burst into flames and crashed, although not before the crew had bailed out. Seeing where they landed Len dashed off with half a dozen *andarte* to round them up.

'They were two of the most arrogant bastards I had ever come across. I told them they had just killed a lot of innocent civilians including women and children, but the pilot showed no remorse at all. He even demanded that I salute him as an officer of the *Luftwaffe*.'

77

To cap it all, they then started quoting the Geneva Convention to Len, who responded by saying, 'The Greeks around here have never heard of it,' and promptly handed them over to Zervas' *andarte* for trial. Len was sure they would be shot, but in the event Woodhouse prevailed upon their captors to keep them as prisoners. Both subsequently escaped.

Before Jordan's arrival Len had earned the sobriquet 'Kyros Yatros' — literally, Mr Healer. It had started when a Greek brought in his son with a badly mangled hand after he had been playing with a detonator. Len had no medical kit but remembered some of the first aid taught him by the cook on the *Dove*. 'We had some bananas so I wrapped the boy's hand in the rotting skins and bound it up. In a few days, although the hand was still a mess, all the inflammation had gone and it had started to heal.'

Len's medical skills were to be tested once more after the bombing of Voulgareli. A number of wounded were brought to him. One was a girl of about fifteen with her stomach slashed open by shrapnel. 'Her parents were in a hell of a state, but the girl just looked at me with these great black eyes and hardly made a sound when I did a bit of probing.' Len had no morphia so gave her 'a good slug of ouzo [local spirit]'. Having got out his Army issue sewing kit, with its normal needle and cotton, he proceeded 'to sew together the bits that looked as if they ought to be sewed together'. The girl recovered. Len met her again in Voltos when he was back in Greece in 1948. 'She was married, but sadly had no children, so maybe I didn't sew up all the right bits.' He did, however, have some difficulty explaining to his wife, who was with him, why an attractive young woman should throw her arms around his neck.

Len also recounts how a mother walked for three-and-a-half days over the mountains with her daughter to consult him about the daughter's period pains. Len's knowledge of such matters was minimal. 'I knew bugger all about female periods except they were a nuisance.' Still he had a reputation to keep, so, with a straight face, prescribed two pills a day before the period was due and one a day during the period. Two months later the woman walked over the mountains again and hugged him to her bosom for curing her daughter. 'She gave me two chickens. The medicine? All I had to give her were water-sterilizing tablets.'

The Germans had a virtually impossible task in protecting their lines of communication in Greece. The mountainous terrain confined road and rail links to the gorges and valleys or along the coastal plains. This meant that such links were few and always vulnerable to partisan attacks at almost any point. There were hundreds of culverts, bottlenecks and bridges offering ideal targets for the *andarte*, who were able to strike and retire quickly into the hills. Myers knew the Allied plan for 1943 envisaged an invasion of Sicily as a stepping-stone to the boot of Italy. He also believed that, eventually, a landing on the Greek mainland was possible. If it came, it seemed probable that Italy would provide the base from which to launch an invasion on to the west coast. Part of his planning for ANIMALS was to encourage the Germans to believe that such an attack would come before any assault was launched on Sicily.

The enemy had only two routes along which to reinforce the west coast. The first was across the high Pindus chain of mountains in central Greece. The road that took this line left Kalambaka and wound through tortuous defiles and passes, including the Metzovo Pass, to Yannina. There it forked, one road running down through Epirus to the coast opposite Corfu, while the other plunged south through more mountains to Arta.

To Len's delight, after the arrival of Warrant Officer Smith, he was allowed to be attached to Barnes's team attacking the northern roads that forked south and west from Yannina into Epirus. Myers was later to write of the success in this area during the latter half of 1943 in the following terms:

'Through Epirus, where Tom Barnes had carefully prepared a most comprehensive plan of sabotage, the results of his and several officers untiring leadership night after night were so brilliantly successful, and the consequent disruption of communications was so complete, that the enemy came to the conclusion that the west coast of Greece was already in imminent danger of being invaded by the Allies.'[21]

Len was out with Barnes night after night, cutting bridges, culverts and telephone lines, ambushing convoys or shooting up German garrisons. 'Oh yes, it was exciting, but I still had to meet the wireless schedules so I was a bit short of sleep. Tom didn't seem to need any so I didn't get much sympathy.'

During this time with Barnes Len witnessed an atrocity that he has never forgotten, perpetrated not by the Germans or Italians, but by communist *andarte* under Aris. Aris had arrived at a village that Barnes and Len were visiting to hold court. One prisoner was a young woman who was dragged weeping and wailing into the village square, where she was stripped naked and tied to a chair with chains. Her crime — eating some of the food she had been sent to collect from the village. Barnes and Len, outnumbered twenty to one, could only watch helplessly as the girl was beaten unmercifully until her back and chest were little more than raw flesh. Then Aris personally untied her before throwing her contemptuously to the waiting *andarte* for a pack rape. Len was physically sick.

There was another incident that upset him. This occurred during the winter of 1943 and involved British personnel. Although Len was not an eyes witness, the story of what happened was common knowledge at the time. Operation ANIMALS had collected a number of 'strays' who had got left behind when the British withdrew from Greece in 1941. One of these was an old sweat private soldier called Tommy. Until recently Len described what happened thus:

'Tommy was pretty useless, but he wasn't a bad bloke even if he did get pissed a lot on *ouzo*. He was with one of the new officers who had come in for Op ANIMALS, a right bastard who would have been more at home in the Nazi army. Anyway, he shot and killed Tommy for what he called insubordination, and all Woodhouse did was send him out of Greece. In my book it was murder and the bastard got away with it.'

It was an object lesson, as Len now readily admits, of making judgements without knowing the true facts. The truth, which Len did not learn until 1987, was somewhat different. Tommy had been drunk during an engagement with the Germans and had thus endangered his comrades' lives. Nevertheless, Woodhouse had travelled half across the country, charged the Major with murder, to the officer's utter incredulity, and got him out of Greece on one of the supply planes which were by then landing on their improvised airstrip. In Cairo doctors diagnosed a cerebral haemorrhage, so the Major was unfit to plead.[22]

Operation ANIMALS was an undoubted success, although it provoked a savage German reaction. On the night of 16 September the Germans burned the town of Kalambaka and launched a major sweep through the mountains into Thessaly and Epirus. Shortly afterwards, on a trumped-up pretext, ELAS attacked Zervas' forces where Barnes and Len provided liaison. 'At the same time the Germans had a go at us too. It was a novel situation being shot at by your own side as well as the enemy.' On 9 October all-out civil war broke out between Zervas' republicans and the communists.

In March, 1944, Len, sitting in the radio shack with the headphones over his ears, was electrified by a 'Flash' prefix to a message from Cairo — the highest priority in the signals book of words. It was addressed to Myers' headquarters, but copied to other outstations of the mission in Greece. It listed half-a-dozen names of people who were on both the Germans' 'Most Wanted List' and the ELAS (communists) 'Death List'. Len was on both. Following it was a short list of three who were to be evacuated within forty-eight hours. Sergeant Willmott was one. What Len did not know until months later was the fact that his efforts in Operation ANIMALS had earned him his second decoration, the Military Medal. The recommendation, signed on 20 September, 1943, contains the following passage:

'Throughout ANIMALS operations the work of Brigadier Myers' wireless personnel often passed unnoticed. Under active service conditions — and most trying ones at that — often in danger Sergeant Willmott's work was of the very highest order.

During the past two months Sergeant Willmott's station has been repeatedly bombed by the enemy. His personal courage and devotion to duty have been exemplary throughout the most trying and dangerous conditions. On at least two occasions Sergeant Willmott has continued to operate his set while actually being bombed.'

Len was not sorry to go, and he had one very private secret. The previous October, using the personal communications system known only to wireless operators, he had transmitted a coded signal to Cairo with the request that it be relayed to London to a Miss Connie Crossland. It simply said, 'Happy 20th birthday. Will you marry me?' The reply was the shortest signal he had ever decoded. It contained one word of text.

On 15 March, 1944, Len waded out to a rubber dingy, embarked in a Motor Torpedo Boat which roared off towards Italy at 35 knots. He pulled a much-thumbed message out of his battledress pocket before settling himself out of the wind. He was going home. He had been in enemy-occupied Greece for two weeks short of eighteen months.

CHAPTER SIX

SOME HONEYMOON

'It's an odd thing about my time behind enemy lines — it never bothered me that I didn't understand the language. . . . Yes, in Greece I learned Greek, but that was because I had a sleeping dictionary. I was married when I went to France.'

When Len returned home in the spring of 1944 it was to a vast armed camp. Everywhere he went, everywhere he looked it was the same — tens of thousands of trucks, tanks, guns and aircraft; hundreds of thousands of troops packed into temporary camps all across southern England. Many of them were American. The only topic of conversation was the 'second front' — the coming invasion of France and the subsequent struggle to liberate Europe. To say activity was feverish was hugely to understate the situation. Preparations and planning for the largest amphibious assault the world had ever seen — or is ever likely to see — were nearing their final phase. SOE was to play a vital part. Len was to become a minuscule cog in the mammoth machine.

After such a long spell of active service, he was disappointed that Baker Street only gave him a week's leave, warning him that he was to stand by for another operation. There was just sufficient time to squeeze in a splendid reunion lunch at Claridge's with Bill Jordan, whom he met by accident at Baker Street. Their animated voices reminiscing in Greek aroused the curiosity of the diners at a nearby table. A man approached them. 'His Majesty the King of the Hellenes wonders why two British soldiers are speaking Greek, and would be greatly interested to meet you.'

'It was quite a lunch party. The King was a nice man and interested in what we had to tell him, although Bill did most of the talking. Bill was never one to mince his words and, king or no king, he didn't mince them now, particularly about the communists. Some of his staff were horrified at Bill's language, both in Greek and English, but the King didn't seem to mind. And he was too polite to say anything about our rather informal dress!'

On 22 April, 1944, Len and Connie were married in the Willesden register office, before dashing off for a few days holiday in Scotland. Within a week Len was back at Baker Street being briefed to go into France. It seemed he would be on loan to the *Force Francais d'Interieur* (FFI), controlled by a Colonel Passy, as he was taken to their headquarters building, close to Baker Street, by an English-speaking French officer.

Two hours of briefing followed. Their party was to be three in number: a French major Len knew as 'Patch', and a Welsh-speaking signaller called Taffy Owens. Afterwards Owens took Len to another room and showed him the wireless sets they were to take. One was the usual SOE B2, not unlike the B1 he had used in Greece, but much lighter and more powerful. The other, unmarked, was a set Len had never seen before. He was to be the principal operator on the SOE set and the link to London. Owens was guarded about the other set, merely telling Len he would be receiving messages from London in a special code whch he, Owens, would re-transmit, on what he termed the 'Enigma' set, without decoding them.[1]

Even today it is impossible to be certain precisely what Len's mission was, or how it fitted in to the D-Day planning. As a wireless operator he was only told what he needed to know, the sets he would use, the codes, frequencies, schedules, but not the actual object of the operation. Certainly it was French-controlled, and designed to help the Resistance forces for the coming invasion and subsequent activities to delay, disrupt and distract the Germans. It was to be in Brittany, but the actual date of the landing — Len was told he would be landed by a Lysander aircraft rather than dropped — was uncertain.

There followed a period of postponements, of waiting, of standing by only to be stood down. If this was the French system Len was not impressed. Nevertheless, he used this time to good effect. He complained officially about his lack of promotion. For three years he had been a sergeant, much of it on active service behind enemy lines, for which he had been awarded the BEM and MM. Most of his contemporaries in Cairo or Haifa now outranked him. He had a point.

'I knew that all operations were voluntary, but I was a bit pissed off when I came out of Greece to find people in Cairo who had never seen a shot fired as staff-sergeants or warrant officers. I thought it worth asking, anyway, as it might mean a bit more for Connie if I didn't come back.'

Len was not to know that as far as the Army was concerned he was still only a substantive lance-corporal! Neither did he know until forty years later that the 'typical stuffed-shirt Regular' Myers, his Commander in Greece, had

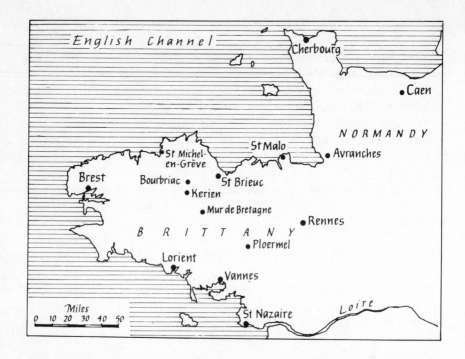

recommended him for a commission.[2] Thus it was a considerable surprise when he was sent for a week or so later to be told to put up the single pip of a 2nd Lieutenant in the General List. This was fine until he discovered that a 2nd Lieutenant's pay was marginally less than a tradesman sergeant. As an added irony his official commissioning date was 11 August, 1944, by which time he he had been back behind enemy lines for three months. Len, however, duly took down his stripes and put up his star, although he was intitially somewhat self-conscious of his unexpectedly accelerated rise in rank. His sister Yvonne remembers him coming round to visit her at Eaton Square to take Connie and her out to lunch. 'Typical Len, he wouldn't take off his mac in case he was saluted.'[3]

Eventually, in late May, he was informed that the Lysander had been cancelled and that they were to parachute in that night. The drop went smoothly. Patch, Owens and Len duly arrived in a soft field near the small town of Mur de Bretagne.

Their reception had been well organized, although Len was amused to find that Owens, speaking Welsh, seemed to be better understood by the Bretons than the French Major. Their first hide was a scruffy farm in a hollow which gave Len problems with reception. Fortunately, within a few days they all moved into a typical French pub in the village which was on higher ground and thus much better for communicating. It also had other facilities. The first floor accommodated the local brothel. Len was newly married, otherwise he might have been tempted to repeat his Greek laundress liaison. He described the girls as a 'pretty decent lot', who used to come up to the attic for a coffee and a gossip with the two wireless operators after their customers had gone.

One of the more embarrassing episodes in Len's career was to follow. Madame offered Len a job, for after the war, as manager of her establishment if he would marry her third daughter. She simply would not believe that one who looked so young could already be married. 'Taffy [Owens] nearly split his sides laughing doing the interpreting.'

Madame, nevertheless, was a kind woman who was forever offering the two signallers wine or coffee. One day Len said he would give a lot for a really good cup of tea. Madame collected a spade and went off into the garden where she carefully counted out some paces before gently lifting some cabbages. Owens and Len watched with keen interest as she returned clutching a tin of Brooke Bond tea. Whatever else she stored in her secret cache under the cabbages Len never discovered, but they were seldom short of some little luxury, which she always offered to Len first with a pleading smile.

The work was dull after Greece. They were confined to the attic for most of the day, only being able to come down after the bar had closed. Even then there was not much to do apart from play bezique, a card game Len never mastered, with a few of the locals. Of the Germans there was little sign, Brittany being considered an unlikely area for the forthcoming invasion, although some convoys passed through along the main road from Brest to Rennes. Sometimes they would stop briefly at the pub for a quick drink or an equally quick trip to the first floor.

Patch, the French officer, lived elsewhere but called in to see them every couple of days, usually with a message to be encoded and sent off to London. To Len there was nothing particularly startling in them; to a wireless operator messages are often just words to be put into code and transmitted. On most nights during his schedule to London, a special message came through, and Owens would transmit it on the other set on a different frequency. Len took a turn sometimes just to vary the operator's signature.

Early in June, a matter of a few days before D-Day, Len's group were moved to Paris, passing from Maquis group to Maquis group by train, lorry, car, or sometimes by bicycle or on foot. The mission? Apparently there was a Maquis uprising planned for Paris at the appropriate moment and another wireless operator was required. To Len it sounded much more interesting than Brittany. He was given a black beret in place of his military side hat, together with a civilian coat to wear over his uniform; then, before reaching the city, Patch told him to hand over his set to the Maquis. Len complied with reluctance on the understanding that it would be safer for a Frenchman to bring it in.

Paris was an anti-climax. Put in a flat on the left bank, forbidden to leave, with no set to operate, he soon become thoroughly bored and disillusioned. These feelings of frustration were magnified tenfold when he heard of the Allied landings on 6 June. History was being made and he was not a part of it. Within a few days, however, his luck turned. He was to return to Brittany, collecting his wireless en route. It was a 'bloody awful journey' which took over three weeks. Now there were road blocks and checks everywhere. He was moved by night and hidden by day — very similar to his escape from Poland although he was now more mature, more experienced, and so less frightened. Most movement was cross-country on foot, or using back lanes and paths away from roads. They hid in isolated farms or woods.

Towards the end of the journey they found themselves with a big group of Maquis in a forest. There was a great deal of excitement and argument, interspersed with expressive gallic gestures, so Len asked his escort what it was all about. The Maquis, it transpired, had information that a troop train from Brest to Paris was expected, and the discussion was on how to shoot it up. Len suggested derailment.

A lot more animated discussion took place, little of which Len understood, until he was asked if he had any experience of explosives.

'I said I had a bit, so they took me down through the forest to the railway. It was a textbook ambush position — the line was cut into the side of the hill on a long curve, with a steep drop on the downhill side, then went into a tunnel.'

The Maquis wanted to blow the tunnel to stop the train, but Len had other ideas. Why not blow the line and derail the train just as it entered the tunnel, then blow the tunnel? He gave them a hand laying the charges before retiring up the hill.

The train, when it came, had half a dozen carriages filled with troops and about a dozen 'flats' carrying tanks. About three-quarters of the train had gone past the charges on the embankment before it went up. It was like a slow-motion movie; the weight of the tank flats dragged virtually the whole train over the embankment. Then the Maquis opened up with everything they had and, at the same time, two very brave Maquisards who had stayed near the railway line blew the tunnel just as the engine was entering it. Chaos and confusion were complete.

'But give the Germans their due, in spite of the shambles and a lot killed or injured, they fought back. Me? I watched from a safe distance in the trees. My job was to look after the wireless.'

Len arrived back in Brittany, at the tiny village of Kerien, at the beginning of August. What was far from clear to him at the time was that he had been earmarked to join what was called Operation ALOES.[4] This mission was under the command of a French Colonel Eono who, with twenty-four others, was to drop into Brittany on the night of 4/5 August to link up with and support SAS teams and JEDBURGH groups, each of which consisted of an Englishman, an American and a Frenchman, of whom two were officers and the third a sergeant wireless operator. Ninety-three such teams were scattered, in uniform, all over Brittany and central and southern France during the summer of 1944. Their tasks were to provide a general staff for the local Resistance wherever they landed, to coordinate the local efforts in the best interests of Allied strategy, and where possible to arrange further supplies of arms. Until then it had been the exclusive preserve of SIS.[5]

Brittany was something of a backwater to both the Allies and the Germans as far as the D-Day landings were concerned. The important thing for the Allies was to establish a firm lodgement area in Normandy, secure the city of Caen and the port of Cherbourg early, prior to a major breakout into central France and up to the Seine. Brittany sat on the flank of such a breakout, and as such merited attention if only to prevent German formations disrupting the sweep to the Seine. It would be nice to seize the U-boat bases at Brest, Lorient and St Nazaire, perhaps by D+50 as the February forecast of Allied operations had suggested, but it was not critical. In the event Brest did not surrender until 18 September (D+104) while Lorient and St Nazaire were still garrisoned by the Germans on 8 May, 1945, the day the war in Europe ended.

The enemy High Command had never considered an invasion of Brittany from the sea a possibility; it was too far from the British ports. It was consequently held by comparatively few divisions in June of 1944. Responsibility for its defence rested with the German 7th Army which also held the Normandy beaches. Only four infantry divisions were stretched out in coastal defences over the 150 miles from Avranches in the east to Brest at the western tip of the Brittany peninsula. One other infantry division was in the south near Lorient and two parachute divisions were refitting in the centre.

Once it became obvious that the landings in Normandy were not a feint, the battles raging in the bocage around Caen in June and July sucked in reinforcements like an ever-growing whirlpool. Formations such as the parachute divisions that could be spared from static garrison duties were moved eastwards from the peninsula. It was the task of the Maquis and their British and American advisers to delay or disrupt this movement.

To get troops out of Brittany to Normandy necessitated using any of the three west-to-east roads from Brest, which all eventually converged on Rennes, the main nodal point of road and rail communications in the centre of the eastern base of the peninsula. The northernmost of these three was a road and rail link that went via St Brieuc to Rennes, or by road only to Avranches. The central road bisected the peninsula on a west-east line through Mur de Bretagne (passing close to Len's pub of ill-repute) and thence on to Rennes. The southern route went via Lorient, from whence a branch road took it through Ploermel to Rennes. Separating these routes were many kilometres of wooded, hilly country with countless tiny villages and scattered farms. It was the home of a highly motivated Maquis organization. It was also the area of 4 SAS (the French 4th Parachute Battalion operating under FFI), all of whom had parachuted into Brittany by the end of June, where they were joined by several JEDBURGH teams. By the end of July, when Len arrived in the area for the second time, it is estimated that the SAS had mobilized some 30,000 Maquisards throughout the peninsula.

On 1 August the Allied armies finally burst out of the bridgehead at Avranches. Lieutenant-General 'Blood and Guts' Patton poured his US 3rd Army through the gap. By 3 August Major-General Middleton's US VIII Corps was on the outskirts of Rennes. His 4th Armoured Division was approaching the gates of Vannes, while the dispirited units of the Germans' XXV Corps dashed for the shelter of the major ports. His 1st Airborne and 1st Infantry Divisions were ordered to head straight down the centre of Brittany to Brest. A year later General Eisenhower was to attribute much of the success of these operations to the activities of the Maquis with the following words:

> 'As the Allied columns advanced these French forces ambushed the retreating enemy, attacked isolated groups or strongpoints, and protected bridges from destruction. When our armour had swept past them they were given the task of clearing up the localities where pockets of Germans remained, and of keeping open Allied lines of communication. . . .'[6]

Len linked up with ALOES at Kerien, in the village school which became the headquarters of the mission. ALOES was the largest of the SOE teams to be dropped into Europe, twenty-eight or thirty strong (the exact numbers are uncertain as the composition of the team kept changing right up to the last minute), but its purpose was clear as set out in FFI Operation Order No. 22 dated 1 August, 1944.

'Resistance HQ for Brittany, under command of Colonel Eono (Mission ALOES), will proceed to the field shortly. This HQ will be equipped to provide internal communications to the five Departments in Brittany: Finisterre, Côtes-du-Nord, Morbihan, Ille and Vilaine, and Loire Inférieure'.[7]

It was a curious mixture of people. Colonel Eono was French, and so was his chief-of-staff, the legendary Colonel Passy, (chief of de Gaulle's Secret Service); the senior British officer was Colonel Stevens, postwar to become a director of the Bank of England, and there were at least two American officers. The signals detachment was commanded by a Swiss-born Dutchman, Captain Hermann André Schoofs, who had been recruited into MI 6 from his hotel in the French Cameroons, and commissioned into the British Army, the remainder being a mixture of French and British. Thrown in for good measure were a Major and a Sergeant from MI 6, a couple of other SOE JEDBURGH teams, and Major Elwes with additional and unnamed SAS personnel. 2nd Lieutenant Willmott was described as the second-in-command of the signals detachment, although he was unaware that this was his job until he was shown the SOE reports in 1988.[8]

This strange assortment of personnel, less Len who was already on the ground, took off in Stirling aircraft from RAF Harrington on the night of 4/5 August. The drop was made successfully south-west of Bourbriac with the exception of the JEDBURGH (DANIEL) team that, for some inexplicable reason, landed fifteen miles from the designated drop zone. Major Wise, JEDBURGH (team FREDERICK) was responsible for their reception. He had earmarked the village school, two cars, and a farm to accommodate the personnel. Wise personally met Colonel Eono in the field shortly after he had landed. Wise, who had been led to expect about six men, was taken aback by the arrival of thirty. There was some confusion on the ground because of this, but fortunately no enemy appeared.

The following morning Wise was therefore somewhat perturbed when he went to the school:

'The mission HQ at Kerien was of no small interest to the villagers as it bore a strong resemblance to a madhouse. I was also a little disconcerted when on entering the school Colonel Eono asked me who I was and what I wanted. In view of the fact that our team had made the entire arrangements for his welfare, and I had introduced myself to him the night before, this was a little staggering.'[9]

Their first task that morning (5 August) was the collection of nearly 200 stores containers that had been dropped in the dark. This proved difficult. There was an urgent need for the wireless equipment but the containers were spread over a wide area, making the task of locating them difficult and dangerous. Nevertheless, their first schedule with London was met. Len was given special responsibility for communications with other JEDBURGH teams in the area.

The following day the entire force at Kerien was in action. A warning was received that a force of some 200 Germans was approaching the village from the south-west. It was later discovered they belonged to the 2nd Parachute Division. The enemy appeared to be unaware of the proximity of the Maquis as they were moving slowly along a minor road, using horse transport commandeered from local farms. Apparently they were making their way towards St Brieuc, unaware that the Americans were much closer — they took St Brieuc later on 6 August. Led by Colonel Passy, the small garrison of twenty Maquisards and fifteen officers from ALOES hastily prepared an ambush. Len relished the idea of a fight as a change from signalling.

The Germans were surprised by the opening bursts of fire and preferred to scatter rather than fight through. They left behind three dead, one of whom had killed himself rather than be captured, four wounded prisoners, plus eighteen cartloads of equipment. The two French guides who had probably been forced to lead the column were also shot dead. Len and the other signals personnel all took part in the action, having previously safeguarded their equipment by hiding it before the battle. All came under fire and conducted themselves properly, with the exception of Sergeant [. . . .] who, in the confusion of the battle, left his crystals and the signals plan in a hedge contrary to his orders.[10]

Later that day the mission at Kerien became involved with trying to get a White Russian unit entrenched around St Brieuc airfield to surrender to the FFI. The Russians declined. Shortly afterwards they were attacked and destroyed by the advancing Americans. On 7 August contact was made with the headquarters of the US 3rd Army. Advanced elements of the Americans were now in the area which allowed them to hand over transport, petrol and captured arms and ammunition to the Maquis.

The next day the decision was taken to move the mission headquarters to Mur de Bretagne, slightly in advance of the main American advance, where they would be useful in providing information to the US 3rd Army, and later to assist the Maquis in keeping open the Americans' lines of communication, or the mopping up of groups of isolated Germans. Len was reluctant to return to 'Madame's' for a number of reasons. Security was one concern, as it was never wise to use the same hide twice, but more particularly there was the threat of the dreaded daughter.

Until ALOES was finally withdrawn on 23 August Len was largely on his own, moving every two or three days, but always within a radius of a mile or so from Mur de Bretagne. He saw Colonel Stevens regularly; other officers also brought him messages to transmit, or picked up those he had received, but, as usual, he was not kept informed of the tactical situation. He was even unaware of the code name of the mission. Not even the colourful character of his Commander, Captain Schoofs, was known to him at the time. Schoofs, whose remarkable wartime career included the capture of a 15,000-ton German ore carrier off the West African coast, found Len's work outstanding. In his report Schoofs described Len as 'an excellent wireless operator, reliable, with a good technical knowledge [who had] shown great resourcefulness and courage in the field'. He later commended Len for his actions in the skirmish at Kerien.[11]

Colonel Stevens described the signals team as having undoubtedly performed the best service of the mission.[12] He singled out Captain Schoofs and Signalman Galloway (a radio mechanic), who had both jumped into enemy territory without any previous parachute training, for particular praise. He noted:

'Owing to the continuous absence of senior officers from ALOES headquarters Captain Schoofs was left in entire command and achieved very successful results entirely on account of his own initiative and competence.'

That, during the eighteen days the mission was in Brittany, they transmitted eighty messages and received seventy is remarkable. Stevens recommended Captain Schoofs for the OBE, and 2nd Lieutenant Willmott, Sergeant Hannaford and Signalman Galloway for Mentions in Despatches. Schoofs received the MBE.

ALOES personnel were extracted from Brittany on 23 August by MTB from St Michel-en-Grève, about thirty miles west of St Malo. Len's memories of the evacuation are three: the tide race getting out to the MTB in a small boat, the excitement of travelling at 35 knots across a calm and moonlit English Channel and the thrill of anticipation at seeing Connie again.

Back in England he had one surprise which caused him embarrassment, amusement, and perhaps some pride. From Baker Street the French officer who had taken him to the initial briefing for Brittany took him to the new FFI headquarters, then in Bryanston Square.[13] He hung around for half an hour in an outer office before being shown into an imposing room where General de Gaulle was standing. Something was said in French, but the only words he understood were 'Lieutenant Willmott'. The General then pinned a ribbon on his chest and kissed him on both cheeks.

'I felt a proper 'nana, and it was all I could do not to burst out laughing as he had to bend nearly double. I didn't know if I was supposed to kiss him back but, luckily, he didn't give me the chance.'

The ribbon was that of the Croix de Guerre with Gold Star, the second highest grade of the order.

CHAPTER SEVEN

A BRIDGE AND A BENTLEY

'This Resistance bloke told me to swim for it, but me I couldn't swim the length of the municipal baths, much less the Rhine. Then, that evening, we saw this Bentley parked behind a German headquarters, so we borrowed it.'

On 17 September, 1944, less than three weeks after leaving Brittany, Len was about to become airborne again on his way to war. He was sitting in a glider on an airfield in the south of England, deafened by the noise as the huge Halifax bombers revved up as plane after plane, engines screaming at full power, staggered into the sky. Each with their ungainly tow, the aircraft turned to join the vast armada forming up for Operation MARKET-GARDEN. It was the start of Field-Marshal Montgomery's plan 'to lay a carpet of airborne troops to seize the bridges over the Rivers Maas, Waal and Lower Rhine', as a prelude to thrusting a spear through the heart of Germany. If it succeeded the war could end before Christmas. Len, however, was worried by more mundane matters:

'It was a bit different to my previous operations. For starters it was daylight, and I didn't think much of the flimsy plywood contraption I was travelling in. I'd have been a lot happier in something with an engine, and with a parachute.'

Len was about to be caught up in the most spectacular, most ambitiously conceived airborne operation of the war, perhaps of all time. The Allied air fleet flew into Holland protected by 1,240 fighters, while over 1,000 bombers blasted enemy anti-aircraft batteries along the route or around the dropping zones. To give an idea of the scale of this operation, the first lift on 17 September for the 1st British Airborne Division and the 1st Polish Parachute Brigade required 161 parachute aircraft plus 320 aircraft towing 320 gliders. Altogether, on this day alone 4,600 aircraft of all types took part. That the execution of the operation did not live up to the brilliance of its conception is history, but for bitter, bloody infantry fighting Arnhem has few equals for the British. Five Victoria Crosses were won. On 26 September, after nine

days' continuous fighting, barely 1,700 survivors out of 9,000 men belonging to 1st British Airborne Division mustered at Nijmegen, along with some 420 glider pilots.[1]

Len was a member of team EDWARD, one of four SOE JEDBURGH inter-Allied teams tasked to provide liaison between General 'Boy' Browning's 1st Airborne Corps and the Dutch Resistance around Arnhem, Nijmegen and Eindhoven.[2] EDWARD was to work alongside corps headquarters; CLAUDE was dropping with the British 1st Airborne Division near Arnhem itself; CLARENCE went with the US 82nd Airborne Division south of Nijmegen, while DANIEL accompanied the US 101st Airborne Division seizing bridges north of Eindhoven.

Each team consisted of a commander and a second-in-command; in the case of EDWARD Captain Jacob Staal and Captain McCord Sollenburger, a US cavalry officer, respectively. Staal was a thirty-one-year-old Dutch-born South African attached to the Queen's Own Dorset Yeomanry, seconded to SOE — quite a mixture. The other two team members were wireless operators, in this case 2nd Lieutenant Willmott and Technical Sergeant John Billingsley of the US Signal Corps. EDWARD was to land SW of Nijmegen, near the village of Groesbeek, alongside corps headquarters. Their landing zone was within a mile of the German border.

The huge air fleets formed up, rank after disciplined rank in the sky; fighter aircraft circled watchfully, now and then darting in or out to shepherd a laggard into position. It was an astonishing sight, although Len could see little from inside his cramped glider. The flight was uneventful, just a bit bumpy over the coast when the flak started firing. He saw one glider hit and disintegrate into chunks of flaming wood. Again he wished he had a parachute. Then, within a matter of minutes, his aircraft was cast off from its tow.

'The sudden silence was eerie. We circled down until we hit the ground with a hell of a thump, bounced several times before finally skidding into a tree and knocking off one wing.'

There were gliders all over the place, some with their tails in the air, some upside down, some burnt out, most damaged in some way. The area was also littered with parachutes. Fortunately, in Len's aircraft there was no fire, and although everyone was shaken and bruised they were able to hack their way out, pleased to find that their jeep and trailer had also survived. The time was 2.10 p.m. on 17 September.[3] Enemy opposition to the landing was reported as slight. A few prisoners were taken.

The next ten days were to be the most exhausting, but perhaps the most rewarding, in Len's long war. EDWARD, at corps headquarters, had a critical role to play anyway, but as events unfolded it was Staal's team, in which Len was the key communicator, that was destined to provide the sole link, not only to the Dutch Resistance, but also to the beleaguered 1st British Airborne Division at Arnhem. One of the contributory factors in the overall failure of the Arnhem operation was the lack of wireless communications between formations. Insufficiently powerful sets had been provided to the divisions; sets failed to work due to the conditions or damage, with the result that none of the three divisions dropped or landed on the first day could communicate with their corps headquarters. Effective wireless communication was never established with 1st British Airborne Division during its desperate struggle to survive north of the Rhine. On 25 September its orders to withdraw had to be duplicated and taken over the river by messenger. The only wireless set that functioned properly throughout was Len's. This, coupled with the Resistance telephone and clandestine wireless networks, prevented a total communications blackout.

As Staal drove his team north into a small wood Len had little idea of their location. Staal and Sollenburger disappeared with the jeep to make contact with the nearest Resistance group, leaving Len and his American signaller, Billingsley, to make wireless contact with London. Their first message was passed at 8 p.m.[4] London had received nothing from the teams with the three airborne divisions. Len tried everything to raise them without success. All he knew was that they were supposed to land near Nijmegen but everything was happening so quickly, pressure on establishing communications was so intense, that he had no time for anything else. His understandable attitude had been: 'I was never particularly fussed about where precisely we were going. That was the team commander's job. My all-important task was to see he had the communications he needed.'

EDWARD had landed close to the village of Groesbeek some five miles south-east of Nijmegen, alongside the Airborne Corps Headquarters. It was thickly wooded, hilly country with the German border and the huge Reichswald forest only a couple of miles to the east. Nearby also were the dropping and landing zones of the US 82nd Airborne Division whose tasks included the seizing of the Groesbeek ridge, the bridges over the River Maas and, last of all, the Nijmegen bridge.

The next nine days were a blurred nightmare. With Staal and Sollenburger co-ordinating Resistance activities Len and Billingsley spent their time coping with an endless deluge of messages to send, receive, encode and decode. It went on day after day, night after night, sometimes on the move, sometimes under shellfire. There was no let-up. The worst part was, according to Len, lack of sleep. 'At times I was staggering around like a doped-up zombie.'

It started on the first night when the team made contact with 300 of the Dutch Resistance in Groesbeek. On D+1 (18 September) they moved, along with Airborne Corps Headquarters, deeper into the woods. Staal organized a patrol into Groesbeek to try to commandeer local transport for corps headquarters. In this he was unsuccessful, but contact was made with more Resistance fighters in Malden. A meeting was set up with guerrilla leaders from the villages of Malden, Heuman, Overasselt and Mook.[5] Most significant of all, telephone communication was established with partisans in Nijmegen, which was still firmly in German hands. Valuable information on the military situation in the town, on the defences of the railway, and of road bridges across the Waal was obtained and given to corps headquarters. It was also established that the CLARENCE team working with the US 82nd Division in the area had lost its set and had two of its party wounded. Len was detailed to handle its traffic as well.

D+2 saw corps headquarters and the EDWARD team on the move again to just south of Nijmegen. It also witnessed two crucial events. At a meeting of Resistance leaders various activities were co-ordinated to assist with the forthcoming attack on the Nijmegen bridge next day. Then, through the local Resistance, a telephone link was established with the Resistance in Arnhem. It was a tenuous link, but the only one of any sort with the besieged British 1st Airborne Division. Vital messages were passed from the Corps Commander, Browning, to the Divisional Commander, Major-General Urquhart. At last intelligence was received on what was happening north of the Rhine.

One 20 September contact was made with the advancing 30th Corps. Staal arranged for its senior Royal Engineer officer to make telephone contact with the Dutch Chief Engineer of Waterworks and Ferries in Nijmegen.[6] The British officer was none other than Colonel (he had dropped a rank since leaving Greece) Eddie Myers, whom Len knew well. Again, throughout the day, the only link anybody had with Urquhart in Arnhem was EDWARD's underground telephone link. The Nijmegen bridge finally fell to a combined assault from the Americans, who had crossed downstream of the bridge on the north bank, and the British Guards Armoured Division crossing the bridge itself from the south.

The mission had moved once more, this time into the St Anna Hospital on the outskirts of Nijmegen. Jacob Staal recruited two girls for code and cipher work. It was Len's job to teach them and in different circumstances he would have found it a pleasure. But the strain was beginning to tell. 'Signals traffic was so heavy that requests had to be sent to London to reduce the flow to the absolute essentials.'

By D+4 Staal's signal office was in contact, through the remarkable Underground telephone system, not just with Nijmegen and Arnhem, but with Amsterdam, the Hague, Rotterdam, Utrecht, Geertruidenberg and Gouda. The Elst came on the line and an eyewitness report of the landing of the Polish Parachute Brigade came through, which had to be relayed to corps headquarters and London. These laconic, unadorned extracts from Staal's Mission Report, emphasize the demands made on the two signallers, Len and T/Sergeant Billingsley.[7] Apart from brief catnaps, neither had had any sleep for nearly four days.

'By then I was pretty well on automatic pilot on the morse key, but Jan [Staal] had even less sleep than I had. He was incredible.'

But this was only the beginning. By the morning of D+5 there had still been no contact with CLAUDE, the SOE team 1st Airborne, so Staal decided to go to Arnhem — rather easier said than done as the Lower Rhine was between them and their destination, not to mention a large number of German troops. In the event heavy enemy fire forced them to abandon the attempt.

The following day, D+6, 23 September, Staal tried again, this time with better results. As his after-action mission report states:

'With great difficulty we managed to cross from Nijmegen to the south bank of the River Rhine opposite the position of the 1st Airborne Division with which no contact had been made yet except through underground telephone. The whole area was under heavy fire and a crossing to the 1st Division proved impossible.'[8]

D+7 was a frantic day. Contact was made with a variety of Resistance groups to sort out difficulties between rival factions. Then a rendezvous was arranged with an officer of the Dutch Intelligence Service at Oudenhoof in the Ressen-Bemmel area. This enterprising officer had a network of thirty wireless sets and information offices spread over the whole country. Staal's report merely records, 'We provided him, through Corps HQ, with a set to contact these.' Len's comments are more earthy at having this huge new burden thrust on him. All of his party had now had virtually no sleep for a week.

By 25 September the remnants of 1st Airborne Division were crammed into an ever-shrinking perimeter around the village of Oosterbeek, on the Rhine just west of Arnhem. The division was fighting a losing battle for its life. Neither the Poles, who had dropped just south of the river on 21 September, nor the 43rd Wessex Division which had fought its way forward from Nijmegen, had been able to reinforce it. That day, D+8, the fateful decision was taken that what was left of 1st Airborne Division must withdraw over the river to the south. As part of this plan the 4th Dorsets were to cross from the Driel area in assault boats that night, to hold the north bank to allow the defenders to get back over the river. Going with them were two sets of two letters, one from the Corps Commander, the other from the GOC 43rd Wessex Division explaining the withdrawal plan. One set went with an officer of the Dorsets, the other was carried by Colonel Myers.

Len has no clear recollection of how team EDWARD crossed the Rhine going north, but getting south again was an adventure impossible to forget. Nevertheless, cross they did, probably as part of the Dorsets' operation. A Dutch Resistance report, compiled in November, 1944, states:

'Captain Staal wanted to establish contact after their arrival in Nijmegen with the Resistance in Arnhem. As this did not succeed, they went over the bridge from Nijmegen to Arnhem. By roundabout routes they arrived in Driel, straight through enemy occupation, and in Driel managed to make contact with the Polish Parachutists who were already there.

'Crossing the river in DUKWs [Amphibious Personnel Carriers] they came in contact in Arnhem with the Allied 1st Airborne Division that was there, and supplied important information about the organization and developments of the operations. During the whole operation and by the fact of crossing the river in boats, they were under very heavy artillery fire.

'The 2nd Lieutenant Willmott and Sergeant Billingsley served as radio operators in the department of Captain Staal. They had constantly to clean their transmission sets from the sand and dirt which explosions caused. Without interruption they remained always in action. Their transmission was excellent both in sending and receiving in which is included decoding of messages in code.'[9]

This report went on to recommend decorations for all EDWARD team members. In September, 1946, Queen Wilhelmina signed the approval of the award of the Netherlands Bronze Lion to 2nd Lieutenant L. R. D. Willmott for 'Exceptional gallantry, leadership, ability and tenacity of purpose, displayed during the operations of the First Airborne Division near Arnhem in September 1944; after landing in enemy-occupied territory he fulfilled his task in an excellent manner'.[10] This decoration is the second most senior award for gallantry in the gift of the Dutch monarch, ranking after the Order of William of Orange, the Dutch equivalent of the Victoria Cross. Only 2,000 Bronze Lions were awarded in the Second World War, under twenty to non-Dutch nationals.

Typically Len makes light of his efforts. The events of those days were a blur of movement, shellfire, keeping the wireless going, constant meetings with Dutch partisans, but above all morse, morse and more morse, coding and decoding incoming and outgoing messages.

'It says a lot for boys' training. Of course the adrenalin was running, but morse had become a subconscious language. One could, and did, send and receive in one's sleep.' RuBBISH -
WHAT SLEEP ANYWAY!!

Team EDWARD's key role as the only link with 1st Airborne Division, and the clearing house for the Dutch underground telephone system, quite apart from their determination to get to Arnhem, was an astonishing achievement by four men who had only met each other the day before they landed.

On 26 September EDWARD team members were on the wrong side of the Rhine near Arnhem. A mile or so to the west a fraction of the decimated remnants of 1st Airborne Division were struggling to swim the river, while the great majority were forced to surrender. As is clear from Len's remark at the beginning of this chapter, swimming was not an option for him.

Staal disappeared into Arnhem to check on the situation, in particular to try to locate a boat. It was a fruitless task. They were trapped north of the river. Just as they were about to pull out of their hide in a ruined house a German convoy trundled down the road to stop outside. For the next four hours they crouched on the remnants of the first floor, hardly daring to breathe, until finally the Germans with much shouting by NCOs went on their way.

Then they had a stroke of astonishing luck. On the outskirts of Arnhem they saw what was clearly a German headquarters and, in the courtyard, a number of parked staff cars. One was a low, gleaming Bentley Vanden Plas with the insignia and flag staff of a German general or senior functionary.[11] They hid their jeep and waited until dark. Sentries patrolled at either end of the car park but, surprisingly, not at the gate.

'We had a quick look round and decided on the Bentley because we reckoned the Germans wouldn't shoot at it as a general's car, and the British wouldn't because it was a Bentley. Unfortunately, the first Allied troops we ran into were Yanks and they didn't understand these things'.

Staal had reservations about being able to start the Bentley without a key. Len, who had had a good look round the Embassy Rolls during his pre-war driver training in Paris, remembered that in a Rolls Royce the ignition switch is a knob, and the key only locks the ignition. From their quick look Len was sure the Bentley was the same, and the ignition switch was not in the locked position.

Just before dawn on 27 September, 'We went back and collected it.' Len was right; the ignition was unlocked. The 3½-litre engine purred into life at the first touch of the starter button. There was no challenge as they pulled away.

With Staal driving they made their way cautiously through the rubble of Arnhem towards the bridge. They had set fire to their jeep and trailer during the night, and with it any lingering hope of escaping to the north. Now they had wheels again.

'I know it sounds dramatic, but it wasn't really — just brass neck and a lot of luck. There wasn't another way out.' They reached the bridge at about 8 a.m. and, hearts in their mouths, joined the procession of vehicles going south. Sentries at either end of the bridge saluted, to be acknowledged by Len in the front passenger seat. 'I'd put on my blue side hat which I always carried in my pack, and I suppose it looked a bit like the German equivalent.' It was a slow journey, overtaking convoys of military vehicles where they could, sometimes being waved through, but anxious not to show too much haste.

At a halt in the traffic Staal and Len changed over. The strain and lack of sleep was beginning to tell; Staal was close to exhaustion. The two Americans had gone to sleep in the back. About five miles south of the bridge they came on a German roadblock where a sentry waved them down.

'What now?' Len asked.

'Ram it,' answered Staal through clenched teeth.

The surge of power, the exhilaration, is something Len will never forget.

Bullets, Germans, everything else was forgotten, except the sheer joy of being behind that long shimmering bonnet with the winged B on the front.

'I must have hit the barrier at about 50 m.p.h. It just snapped like matchwood, although it bent the bonnet a bit. The sentries jumped out of the way and we were through before they knew what happened.'

A few shots were fired after them but none, as far as Len knows, actually hit them. The road was clear so Len kept his foot down. A mile or so further on they were greeted by burst after burst of machine-gun fire, but this time from in front. Len slammed on the brakes and they all jumped into a ditch.

'We found a handkerchief that had once been white and cautiously poked it up, shouting "Allies, Allies" — I was shouting "British" at the top of my voice. The firing stopped and we carefully surfaced and tied the handkerchief to the flag mast.'

The engine was still running, but the car looked like a kitchen colander. The first person they saw was a large black American top sergeant. All he said was, 'Jeeessus where'd you guys spring from?' He then offered cigars all round.

After brief calls at the US 82nd Airborne Division and 1st Airborne Corps they drove to Brussels where the Dutch Resistance headquarters was based in the Olympic Hotel. The usual debriefing followed, and 'a bit of a party, but only a bit of a party — we were too damn tired'. Next morning Len was told he was flying back to London.

Six days later he parachuted back into occupied Holland.

On the third day after his return Len was taken to the Dutch section of SOE, based in a side street near Bryanston Square. There were only two being briefed — Len and a Dutch officer he knew as Hans or 'Hank' van Gehlen. Van Gehlen's task was to set up an escape route for Dutch Resistance and for Allied servicemen cut off after Arnhem. Len was to be his wireless operator. This was to be the only operation that worried him from the outset. As he later explained:

'I was always shit-scared in the plane before a drop, but I had always been perfectly okay once I was out the door and on the ground. This time it was different. I was really frightened, more a sort of nagging fear, particularly at the length of time I was compelled to spend on the set. It was even worse for Hank; at least I had a few quiet times when I could pull myself together.'

Much of this apprehension was caused by the knowledge that Dutch Resistance had been penetrated, which meant the awful uncertainty as to whether betrayal was just around the corner. Additionally, this was to be Len's only operation when he was, of necessity, to spend considerable time on his own. In Greece, Brittany, or on the Arnhem operation, there had always been plenty of partisans looking after the mission, or even Allied troops nearby. His briefing had added to the unease. Thee was a strange atmosphere, an air of hesitation and uncertainty that had set his imagination on edge.

In view of Len's worries it is worth having a closer look at what the job of an operator entailed, his problems, and the risks he ran. As we have already observed, fifty years ago wireless communication lacked all of today's sophisticated gadgetry, orbiting satellites and burst transmissions. There was no voice communication, except by S-phone over short distances, so reliance was placed entirely on morse and manual coding or decoding. Even with skilled operators like Len, lengthy messages could take hours to send or receive.

The wireless Len took into Holland the second time was the B 2 set. It weighed 30lbs and was carried in a suitcase about two feet long. Although it had a wide frequency range its signal was weak, as such a set could not generate more than 30 watts of power. An equally serious problem was the length of the aerial — some seventy feet. How to erect it so as to be effective and concealed at the same time was often insuperable. Every operator needed two crystals for his set. Without them it was impossible to transmit. Although small and comparatively easy to conceal, they were, if seen, unmistakable for what they were. Additionally, they broke easily in transit or if badly packed in a drop.

By 1944 the Germans had become proficient in picking up wireless transmissions and pinpointing the probable location. The quickest way to bring the detector van, with its accompanying troops, to the vicinity was to pass a long message. In a large city an operator taking this sort of risk might expect unwelcome visitors within fifteen to thirty minutes. For Len, and others like him, the key to avoiding capture was the diligent, unfailing observance of certain rules: always keep mobile, never use the same site more than once, keep changing crystals and frequencies, keep irregular schedules, always pack up immediately after a transmission, have as little contact with outsiders as possible and, above all, keep messages short. How long is short? While reasonably secure in the mountains of Greece with *andarte* nearby to give warning and protection, there was little need to restrict the length of a message for purely security reasons. In France a twenty-minute transmission would be the maximum for safety, whereas in Holland five to ten minutes was a long message.

Len explained his method thus:

'I tried desperately hard to keep messages short in Holland in particular. If I felt it was too long it was broken down into parts to send at different times, possibly from different hides. There was no set time for skeds [schedules]. London was always on listening watch so at the end of a sked I could arrange the time of the next one. It was never possible outside Greece to keep to fixed times. If I couldn't come up at the time I said I would, it didn't matter too much as I knew London would be alert, listening for me, all the time.'

As part of an operator's security procedure no signals papers, cyphers or codes were ever taken on an operation. Len carried an ordinary book and 'the code in my head'. In France and Holland he was trained to insert a security check in all his messages. A simple word was included in every transmission; if it was not there it meant something was seriously wrong, probably that he was sending under duress as a captive.

It was rare indeed for a message to reach its final destination precisely as the sender had intended, no matter how accomplished the operator making the transmission. A poorly sited aerial, bad weather, atmospherics, jamming, errors in encoding and shaky morse all had a part in preventing perfection. Also every message had to go through a number of stages, each with its possibilities for error — encoding, transmission, reception, decoding, and then teleprinting — before it was read by the recipient. Making sense of garbled, corrupt texts was an art only acquired with long experience. Even then, how did the receiver know whether an incorrect security check, an omitted codeword, was a genuine mistake by an exhausted man or that the operator was a prisoner?

At his briefing Len was given a most unusual document. It 'gave me a cold feeling in the pit of my stomach'. When he had dropped into France he had carried a card, written in English on one side and French on the other, signed by Generals Eisenhower and Koenig stating his codename and requesting the local population to give him every assistance as a British officer. What he was given for this mission into Holland was quite different. He was handed written authority, signed by General Eisenhower and the then Judge Advocate-General of 21st Army Group, Rayner Goddard (a future Lord Chief Justice of England), to use whatever force he deemed necessary to ensure his orders were obeyed. He was given the ultimate authority to shoot any British soldier who refused to leave Holland and be brought out via the Resistance escape routes.

On the night of 3 October, 1944, Len followed van Gehlen through the side door of a Dakota aircraft north of Arnhem, near the small town of Apeldoorn. He found jumping from these aircraft easy. The air speed was slow, the door was large and 'if you kept your eyes open you saw yourself being swept upwards under the tail, so that you were momentarily higher than the aircraft and could actually look down on it for a fleeting second'. As he floated through the darkness Len could see the buildings of the town of Appeldorn three or four miles away. He said a silent prayer that their reception committee would be Dutch, not German. It was.

The reception party bundled up their parachutes and led them across fields to the outskirts of the town, their aim being to meet up with a resistance leader who was a doctor in Apeldoorn. Well before dawn, leaving Len hiding in a clump of bushes, van Gehlen cautiously approached the doctor's door and knocked. It seemed an age to Len before it was answered, although it cannot have been more than a few moments. Shortly afterwards they were settled in an attic with a cup of steaming ersatz coffee and a small glass of 'that neat firewater the Dutch call a drink. I asked Hank if he wanted me to get through to London, but he said it was too dangerous from that house in case we had been followed. I didn't understand what they were saying so I went to sleep.'

The next night van Gehlen, who seemed to know the area well, led Len to a farm where he set up the radio and made his first contact with London. The following night they moved again. This was to be the pattern of his life for the next ten weeks; never in the same house for more than two days, and never making more than two transmissions from the same place. It was a lonely existence, not unlike his time in Poland except that now he was much more aware of the risks, and he had a specific job to do.

Van Gehlen was out most days, returning in the evenings to where Len was hidden. Sometimes he would just give Len a message for encoding before disappearing again, possibly returning later or the next day to lead him to another hide. Occasionally he would stay while the message was sent; then they would move. Most of their travelling was at night, across country, between isolated farmhouses within a five-to-ten-mile radius of Appeldorn. Only rarely did they travel by car or truck or in daylight.

The messages were principally lists of names or codewords which van Gehlen did not explain, but which Len assumed were references to routes. The names were mostly Dutch, with a number of British and a few Polish. The route or routes followed by the 'packages' (escapees) were unknown to Len as he did not need to know, although he surmised that the majority were got out by sea.

His main concern was the length of the messages. That frightened him, as he was fully aware of the competence of the German intercept organization. He was for ever asking van Gehlen to cut them down. Once or twice he refused to send the whole message, insisting on transmitting it over two nights. 'That caused a bit of a flare up, but the bloke was under terrific strain moving around as much as he did.'

Len's sense of humour often came to his rescue. There were few occasions during the war when he could not see the funny side of soldiering. One evening, just after dusk, van Gehlen and Len arrived at a small farmhouse where he was introduced to a farmer who spoke some broken English. His young wife, 'anything but an oil painting', said nothing and kept in the background. After a meal Len set up his wireless and got a message off to London. Van Gehlen departed saying he would be back in the morning, so Len settled down for the night in a warm corner of the kitchen. Then

'This farmer bloke said, "No, No", and took me up to the bedroom — there was only one, with the usual bloody great Dutch double bed — and insisted that I slept there. Well, I was soon asleep nice and snug under a big duvet, only to wake up with someone else getting in. I thought the wife didn't understand so I started to get up, but she pulled me back making shushing noises. Then I realized she was bollock naked! I tried to tell her I was married, but she just made more shushing noises. It took me a hell of a time to get to sleep.'

He was quite alone when he woke in the morning. He came down to the kitchen not knowing what to expect.

'The wife was cooking breakfast as if everything was perfectly normal and the farmer greeted me with a big grin and, "My wife, she good fuck, *hein*?" I just turned bright scarlet.'

Later Len told van Gehlen about it, but he just roared with laughter and said, 'Maybe the man wants a son'. He only laughed more at Len's protestations of innocence.

One problem that van Gehlen encountered, which he discussed with Len, was the reluctance of some soldiers to escape. Many had fled north after the Arnhem surrender and found themselves billets on farms. The farmers were sometimes equally reluctant to let them go. Most of the young Dutchmen had either been sent to Germany as forced labour or were away from home with the Resistance, so an able-bodied soldier was welcome, often in more ways than one. A number had also been wounded and were cared for by their hosts. A good example of this being General Sir John Hackett who was looked after by the Dutch when, as a Brigade Commander, he was badly wounded at Arnhem.[12]

The problem was compounded by the fact that many of these soldiers had set themselves up, as Len puts it, with 'mobile hot-water-bottles', daughters or wives whose men were away or even dead. These men also knew that the end of the war was in sight. When there was likely to be a problem with one of these soldiers van Gehlen took Len with him. Although there were not many such encounters Len did not enjoy them, conscious as he was of the dreadful authority in his pocket. Not that he had much sympathy for them. As far as he was concerned, 'There was a bloody war on, and these bastards were skiving.'

He admits, however, that they were still Englishmen, and often wondered whether he would have had the courage to carry out the orders he had been given. These 'scrimshankers', as he called them, tried all sorts of dodges. One young fellow pretended he was deaf and dumb. As he turned away Len fired a shot into the ground nearby. The soldier jumped like a startled rabbit and yelled, 'What the fuck . . .?'. Clearly neither deaf nor dumb. Another older man tried to pretend he did not understand English although he was wearing battledress trousers over his clogs. Len read out the 'authority' to him in English, then got van Gehlen to read it in Dutch. The soldier raised his manure fork to shoulder height. Len drew his pistol. It was a long thirty seconds as Len's finger tightened on the trigger. The man lowered the fork and gave no more trouble.

Asked directly if he ever had to use this final sanction Len answers with an equally direct 'No', although he makes it clear that he would have done so had it been necessary. He was twenty-four at that time, old beyond his years and hardened by his experiences — experiences behind enemy lines where the Geneva Convention is not necessarily relevant. Today he will say with a smile, 'You can't really blame them I suppose; that older bloke had a real smasher of a widow, but it was different then.'

In mid-December van Gehlen told Len that the flow of 'packages' was drying up and that he would join the next group out. When the time came to leave he discovered that van Gehlen was staying. Len was furious. 'We had a bit of a barney. I told him that, if he was staying, so was I. Hank insisted that it was a direct order, and anyway he had another job to do as a Dutchman, so after a bit I gave in.'

For about eight nights he travelled across country, initially with an escort of two partisans. Almost every night they picked up one or two escapees, including several Dutchmen. By the time they reached the flat, low-lying coast the party was about ten strong. On the ninth night they all huddled together in an old barn at the edge of some marshland, desperately trying to generate some warmth. Eventually a pinprick of light flashed out at sea. Their guide responded with his torch. There followed an agonizingly cold wade in waist-deep water out to a rowing boat which took them slowly, silently, out to the waiting trawler.

The following night, 19 December, 1944, the trawler docked at Aberdeen. Two days later Len was back in London being debriefed. His questioner was 'very keen to know how van Gehlen was in himself. He also told me that we had got 147 people out — about 40 British, a few Poles and the remainder

Dutch'. Although Len cannot be sure, it is almost certain that on this occasion he was working for the Dutch Secret Service. Certainly it was the Dutch who rewarded him for his efforts; he was awarded the Dutch Resistance Cross — forty-two years later.

Apparently the Dutch authorities had singled him out for this award immediately after the war but had no idea of his whereabouts. In 1985, at an Anzac Day parade in Sydney, Len was among those gathered around the Cenotaph. He was wearing his medals, and the Netherlands Bronze Lion caught the eye of a Dutchman in the contingent. He struck up a conversation with Len, during which his mission at Appeldorn was brought up. His Dutch friend was intrigued and later made enquiries through official channels back in Holland. Eighteen months later, on 31 October, 1986, Len was finally invested with his fifth decoration for distinguished service and gallantry by the Netherlands Ambassador to Australia.

CHAPTER EIGHT

HAPPINESS AND HORROR

'He had a woman with him who must have been Ilse Greise, plus a couple of Alsatians. You'd have had to be deprived of a woman for about ten years to take a second look at her.'

Christmas, 1944, was Christmas with Connie, the best Christmas of Len's life. Christmas, 1939, he had been in Poland, Christmas, 1940, on duty in an underground bunker in St James's Park, Christmas, 1942, and 1943 in Greece. Christmas, 1944, could have been anywhere as far as Len was concerned as long as he was with Connie. In fact it was in his aunt's small house in Harlesden. Len was a happy man. It was also the beginning of the first real leave he had had since the outbreak of war, apart from his brief honeymoon and short interlude behind the enemy lines in Greece.

On 23 January, 1945, their first child, a daughter, was born. Len became a typical proud father, fumbling with nappies, fussing over bottles and generally amazing Connie with his domesticity. As far as wartime restrictions and shortages — and living with an aunt — allowed they both settled down to the thoroughly peacetime activities of caring for baby Shirley. They scarcely noticed how battered London looked after five years of war. Connie had survived the blitz at its worst and was able to ignore the menace of the V1s and V2s, although to Len they seemed a grossly unfair way to wage war.

Their pleasures were simple — walks in the park, exploring nearby street markets or junk shops picking up a few bits and pieces against the day they had a home of their own, visits to the library to change books, or an occasional trip to the cinema. Otherwise they were content sitting in front of the fire with the radio, and Len's books. His passion for reading was another thing that surprised Connie. 'He read anything and everything he could lay his hands on.'

In early 1945 Len had time for reflection. Nine-and-a-half years had passed since he had joined the Army as a boy signaller at Catterick. For the past five years he had lived for the present, day to day, sometimes hour by hour. It did not occur to him that he had done anything unusual or special, nor did he give much thought to the fact that he had been behind enemy lines for something over three of the last five years. In his experience special

12. Officers of 22 SAS, Sungei Besi Camp, Malaya, 1952. From left:
(1) Major Len Willmott, (2) Captain Pat Winter, (5) Lt-Colonel 'Tod'
Sloane, (7) Major Johnny Cooper.

13. Presentation of the Netherlands Resistance Cross, Sydney, 31
October 1986. Len with Connie.

14. On the same occasion, Len with (*above*) Air Marshal Sir James Rowland, KBE, DFC, AFC, Governor of New South Wales, and (*below*) the author.

operations were normal, so he had little or no familiarity with what went on in more conventional military units.

He came to the conclusion that he was a lucky man. He enjoyed his job as a wireless operator and knew that he was good at it. It would not have occurred to him at the beginning of the war that he would have reached commissioned rank at the age of twenty-three. It had been a long way from his thoughts when he asked for promotion before Brittany. Ex-boy soldiers expected to reach the higher non-commissioned or warrant ranks in the Corps; a few, very few, would rise to quartermaster commissions. Now, at twenty-four, he had captain's stars on his shoulders and four distinctive ribbons on his chest. He had come through the war without a scratch, and he had a family — but what next?

By January, 1945, the war was going well for the Allies. Their armies were poised to cross the Rhine to thrust deep into Germany. But there was still Japan. Peace might still be some way away. As a family man now he had to think about the future. The only trade he knew was soldiering, and he was wise enough to know that within that trade his skills covered a narrow field. Wireless would play an increasing part in any army of the future, but his own background and experience did not necessarily fit him for a peacetime army.

Len broached the subject of what they should do after the war. In his aunt's small sitting-room in Harlesden he tried to put forward the options, to explain what staying in the Army might mean.

Len knew, although he had been promoted to Acting Captain on his return from his second drop into Holland, that his commission was 'General List' and 'Hostilites Only'. His substantive rank in the Royal Corps of Signals was still lance-corporal. The likelihood was that if he wanted to stay in the post-war Army, he would have to relinquish his commission, although he was optimistic enough to believe he would end up as sergeant. Connie put an end to any doubts he might have had.

'I told him that I didn't mind if he was a lance-corporal or a colonel. He was a soldier, and a good one. If he wanted to stay that was fine by me. I would go wherever he went. Anyway he was now an officer, the world was going to be a different place after the war, so why didn't he apply for a regular commission? I was a good-looking lass and wouldn't disgrace him in any officers' mess.'

Connie's blunt Yorkshire reasoning made Len determined that when the time was ripe he would apply for a permanent commission. In the meantime he would make some enquiries. Still lurking in the back of his mind was a determination to get back to the SAS. Instinctively he knew that the SAS was the sort of unit he could fit into as a regular officer. He was not to know that they would be disbanded soon after the war.

Meanwhile he remained on leave, reporting in regularly to Baker Street where there was nothing for him until, at the end of February, he was posted as an SOE Air Liaison Officer to an airfield near Thetford in Norfolk. A confidential report in SOE archives dated 20 March, 1945, records him as having 'entered into air liaison work with amazing aptitude'.[1]

Len's comments on his first desk job were not so complimentary.

'That job must have been the joke of the year. Maybe it had been an airfield from which SOE ops were launched, but by the time I got there it was a Mosquito bomber base. I had an office, a telephone which never rang, a typist who had nothing to type, an ancient shooting brake for liaison duties, and fuck all to do.'

Never able to be idle for long, he resumed his long solitary walks, getting to know the country well, particularly the royal estate at Sandringham. Nor did it escape his eye that there were pheasants in abundance. He made friends with 'a right pair of characters', the Catering Officer and the Armaments Officer.

'The three of us used to go off in my old jolopy. I drove; the Catering Officer knew just about every pheasant in the area by name, and the Armaments Officer sat in the back with a .22 rifle.'

The mess was never short of pheasant on the menu, so much so that the complaints book featured a number of entries demanding more varied fare. Even his aunt in Harlesden suggested that a rabbit would make a change.

He had bought an old Norton motorbike — petrol was no problem as it came out of his official car — so he was able to spend most weekends with Connie in London, extending them from time to time by calls on Baker Street.

On one of his periodic visits Len broached the subject of a permanent commission. His application was well received, even encouraged. It is dated 5 April, 1945.[2]

He was medically examined on 12 April by the Medical Officer to MO1 (SP), War Office. He was 'strongly recommended' by a Major with an illegible signature in the Royal Scots Fusiliers whom Len has no recollection of meeting. The Brigade Commander's recommendation stated: 'A very good type who has a remarkable war record'. The special to arm recommendation is signed by Brigadier F. W. Nicholls, Royal Signals, who happened to be serving in SOE, to the effect that the Royal Corps would be happy to have him as a regular officer. He appeared before No. 2 Regular Commissions Board at Hereford on 11 June, 1945. He was graded 'B' (above average).

However, between his medical board on 12 April and the Regular Commission Board on 11 June, there was a short interlude in Len's life which left a lasting scar, one that even now he is reluctant to talk about. Reporting to Baker Street on the day of his medical he was warned for a short notice operation and told to report for a briefing the next day.

It was a very different briefing from any he had had before. To start with he was the only person being briefed, and there were five or six officers in the room, which was unusual. Colonel Buckmaster, the legendary head of 'F' Section, was one, but he did not say anything. Most of the briefing was done by a Major Len had not seen before. The gist of it was that the advancing Allied forces were about to overrun a major prison camp — 'I cannot remember if the term "concentration camp" was used.' He would be given a list of names and would either be landed by Lysander or parachuted in to join up with the leading elements of the Canadian Corps, who had been earmarked to liberate it. His job was to go in with them to check the registers against a list of names he would be given. An older man, sitting to one side, interjected at that stage to emphasise strongly that was all he was to do — just check the registers against the list, report by radio if he could, and get back to London. A Lysander would pick him up.

He got nothing more other than that the operation was extremely sensitive. No, he could not be given a date, but it should be in the next few days. He was to remain in London, and if he went out of the house he was to telephone in to let them know where he was. What he was not told was that SOE were sending him to Belsen concentration camp in which they believed a number of SOE agents were incarcerated. Anyway, it was not Len's job to get them out if they were found there. The next morning he received a telephone call ordering him to report at once, ready to go that night.

Now, nearly fifty years on, there are differences of opinion as to who entered Belsen first. The only certainty is that it was not elements of the Canadian 4th Armoured Division who were specifically tasked to liberate it, but that the dubious honour is shared among several SAS patrols. A number of SAS soldiers went into the camp ahead of the Canadians, who had been held up for forty-eight hours by the still-fanatical Hitler Youth Division. Additionally, an advanced patrol took Len in the day before it was formally liberated. He is one of only three men who spent a night there while it was still under German control.

April, 1945: the Allies were across the Rhine racing east, while the Russians raced west, towards Berlin. The Germans were on the verge of complete collapse, the Allies and the Soviets were staking out territorial claims in eastern Europe that would change the map for another forty-five years. There was no front line as such, German resistance was patchy and uncoordinated. Some units fought hard, even to the death, others surrendered with relief to the first Allied soldier they saw. Only against the Soviets was the fighting protracted and without quarter.

Well out ahead of the advancing armoured columns were the SAS, elements of both British Regiments, 1st and 2nd SAS, some eighty jeep patrols in all; eighty independent patrols operating over a front of a hundred miles or more under the overall command of the illustrious Colonel Paddy Mayne.

At this stage of the war the SAS were given the role of advanced reconnaissance, probing forward at speed identifying German pockets of resistance, shooting their way through if they could, shooting their way out, reporting it, and going round if they could not. Casualties were high. With eighty patrols operating independently few knew where others were at any given time. Officially, in SAS circles, the first to find Belsen was Captain Alex Muirhead commanding A Squadron, who came across it accidentally, although he did not go inside himself. Muirhead has described the problem as he saw at the time:

'Things were moving very swiftly. We had had a set-to with some German half-tracks; Bill Fraser had been hit and I had taken over the squadron. Hackles were up and we were in hot pursuit of the enemy. My assessment of the situation was that I did not have sufficient strength to take over and run the camp. The guards were all for throwing down their weapons and going home. They were also for opening the gates and letting the prisoners out.

'Also, my previous medical training as a student made me fairly certain that typhus, dysentery and other infectious diseases were rife. The prisoners must not be released into the countryside. I was not prepared to risk my men unnecessarily, especially as hospital and other facilities were relatively close behind.

'Finally, I had a fighting job to do and I was not going to be sidetracked. I then called the camp guard commander and spoke to him through one of the Canadians (a German-speaker). I asked him if he had any English prisoners. He said "No". There was in fact one French SOE prisoner, Yvonne Rudellat (Jacqueline) who died in Belsen after the liberation.

'I then told the guard commander that the main British Army was close behind and that if they kept the camp secure they would come to no harm. However, if any of his men left his post or allowed any prisoner to escape I would shoot him and all his guards personally. I added that I would be in the area and would be keeping an eye on him. He was as scared as hell as he had been expecting to be shot from the beginning and was therefore very cooperative. After this we went on our way.'[3]

Muirhead's squadron sergeant-major had been inside briefly, but the man who not only went in but was almost certainly the first British soldier to interrogate the Commandant, the infamous Obersturmbahnführer Kramer and his playmate who made lampshades out of tattooed human skin, Ilse Greise, was Sergeant Duncan Ridler MM.[4] Ridler, who was the Intelligence Sergeant of 1 SAS, was a German-speaker and the leader of a patrol that arrived ahead of the Canadians. His description is vivid and objective:

'A message had come over the radio that the Commandant of a concentration camp wanted to surrender. We had no idea what a concentration camp was at that stage. Also a rumour had been circulating for several days that there were captured SAS in a camp in the vicinity, and we knew of Hitler's orders that all SAS were to be shot out of hand. My patrol was fairly near the grid reference given, so we decided to swing back and have a look.

'About a mile from the camp, as we came through the forest, we ran into a cordon of East European troops. They were an odd-looking lot wearing a sort of orange uniform with brown epaulettes — Bulgarians or Hungarians I think. There were hundreds of them standing almost shoulder to shoulder, but they did not seem to be hostile, which was reassuring. They told us that there had been an outbreak of typhus or typhoid in the camp, and their job was to prevent anyone leaving the area.

'That did not seem to include going in, so we pressed on and came to a high wire fance. The stench hit us even before we saw it. There was an open gate a little way along, with a large group of Germans standing around, including the Commandant; cool as you please, polished jack boots and all, for all the world as if he was leading a welcoming committee. He was a nasty-looking bastard, and there was an even nastier-looking bitch with a couple of Alsatians at heel with him. I was yet to discover just how nasty.

'I asked him in German if there were any British prisoners in the camp. He said "No". It was all very polite and formal, but we were feeling a mite insecure — there were only three of us and a hell of a lot of Germans, all armed. I think I would have pulled out then but there were odd shots going off in the camp, so I told the Commandant to stay where he was and drove in, my gunner with his finger very close to the twin Vickers [machine gun] trigger.

'One of the first things we saw was a huge pile of rotting potato peelings, about six feet across, and a lot of scarecrows grovelling on it. They were barely human. There was a Kraut at a cookhouse window taking casual shots at them, and another a little further away having target practice into one of the compounds at the wretched bundles of rags cowering on the ground. We didn't think it would be a good idea to open fire — the watchtowers were still manned — in case we had a conflagration on our hands. We might have shot our way out but there would have been a wholesale massacre of the inmates. 'But we stopped them firing all right — permanently. Then we got together everything edible from the German cookhouse and loaded it into the jeep and distributed it as best we could. We made the Germans there strip and we gave away their clothes to the prisoners, but most were too weak to put the clothing on. One poor bastard managed to get on a pair of boots, but remained rooted to the spot. He was too weak to lift his feet.

'Then we found the pit. Dear God, I cannot find the words for it even now. And some of them were still moving.

'There was nothing much more we could do, so we drove back to the gate. A British sapper Colonel had arrived with what appeared to be the official take-over party. He spoke no German, believe it or not, and had no interpreter. Kramer, as he proved to be, spoke no English so I had to stay to interpret. I think the Colonel must have been feeling about as insecure as we did, and the Germans were showing signs of being edgy, so it was still very polite and formal, with Kramer anxious to hand over as if he was handing over a holiday camp.

'One thing the Colonel had brought with him was a de-lousing unit. We had only been in Belsen for two of three hours, but we were crawling with lice. We were their first customers.'[5]

Instead of landing in a Lysander Len found out at the airfield that he must jump from a Liberator as the weather was poor. As usual he was able to snatch an hour's sleep before being called forward to the cockpit to try to identify the dropping zone. The pilot came in low as Len peered out into the darkness, looking for five fires set out in the shape of a C. There they were; the navigation had been spot on. The aircraft circled once more. Len jumped.

His reception committee was three British soldiers in a jeep. They wore no badges of rank and nothing to identify their unit. Very little was said. Len and the commander compared map references. The rendezvous with the Canadians was the same, so, dousing the fires and stowing Len's parachute, they cleared the dropping zone as rapidly as possible, hiding up in a wood close to the rendezvous until dawn.

By midday there was no sign of the Canadians, but rather the sounds of a stiff battle going on about four miles to the south. Len realized that the Canadians had probably run into trouble and was worried that the people he had been sent in to identify might be shot before the Canadians got there. Also he had to meet up with a Lysander the next day. He conferred with the team commander. As they had a map reference for the camp they decided to go in on their own.

'We got there in the late afternoon. We could smell it long before we saw it — it was indescribable — the stench just hung in the air like a sticky cloud. The gate was open and a number of guards standing about. We just said "British Army, others coming, where *killandante?*" The guard commander pointed to some buildings inside the perimeter. We pushed on through several other fences and gates feeling pretty bloody exposed with a lot of armed Germans about. The gunner and signaller in the back, however, were looking pretty businesslike.'

The administrative buildings were in the centre of the camp, with the guards' quarters at a right-angle to them. Turning the jeep for a rapid exit and leaving the gunner and signaller hunched over the twin Vickers and the bren gun, Len and the sergeant went into the headquarters building.

'The Commandant, who I know now was Kramer, was an arrogant bastard, but quite polite. He had a woman with him who must have been Ilse Greise, plus a couple of Alsatians. You'd have had to be deprived of women for about ten years to take a second look at her. Kramer sent for an interpreter who turned out to be a Dutch prisoner — he was hollow-cheeked, starved and terrified, but nothing like the scarecrows I saw next morning.

'I asked for the registers of prisoners and Kramer produced them pretty quickly, but my heart sank. It was all in that fancy German script which I couldn't read. The Dutch interpreter was either too frightened, or couldn't read it either. I told the Commandant the main forces would arrive any minute, and the only other thing I did was to tell him and the other Germans in the offices to unload their weapons and pile the ammo on a table. I didn't think they would surrender their arms.'

By then it was dark. Hoping the Canadians wold get there by morning, and not relishing the idea of running the gauntlet of the camp in the dark, they stayed put in the Commandant's office, with the other two on guard outside. It was a long, jittery, uncomfortable night.

In the morning German orderlies brought in tea and black bread. By about 9 a.m. there was no sign of the Canadians and Len had to keep the rendezvous with the Lysander, so he and his group drove out after warning Kramer of dire consequences to himself if any prisoners were killed.

'As we drove out we could see these pathetic bundles of rags hanging on the wire of the compounds or huddled in heaps — and the stench — I can smell it still. But there was nothing we could do.'

About a mile from the gate they met the leading Canadian troops, French Canadians as Len remembers, stopped briefly to tell them what they had seen and 'drove like hell for the RV'. The Lysander was on the ground, Len shook hands with the three soldiers 'who had been so bloody marvellous in the camp when I was scared stiff', and climbed aboard to the pilot's greetings: 'You're lucky, I was giving you five more minutes.'

On the flight back, even during the re-fuelling stop in Brussels, Len could not talk. He had never felt so totally depressed and inadequate.

'I'd achieved nothing, and saved nobody. I'd seen something of German brutality in Greece, but nothing to compare with what I'd seen at Belsen. I wanted to weep, but that didn't come until I got home to Connie. And I couldn't tell her why I was crying.'

CHAPTER NINE

A FUNNY SORT OF PEACE

'There were over twenty, ranging from elderly women to small children. . . . It was a difficult decision deciding who I would take, but I had to give priority to the men who I assumed were the important "parcels". It was heart-rending.'

The Belsen mission was Len's last of the war. He returned to his bomber base near Thetford where he was warned to expect a posting to the Far East, to Force 136, where Japan seemed certain to carry on its fanatical resistance to the bitter end. An invasion of Japan itself was planned. Then, on 6 August, 1945, the first atomic bomb fell on Hiroshima, followed by another three days later on Nagasaki. It was enough. Japan surrendered. For Len it meant the cancellation of his Far East posting. Shortly afterwards his service with SOE ended with a quiet handshake and a few words of thanks from an officer he had never known. There was also a reminder that where he had been and what he had done was to remain secret.

Slowly the enormous administrative task of bringing the troops home and demobilizing them in some semblance of order got under way. SOE's task was greater than most. Over 10,000 men and women were scattered in small groups all over the world, some of whom were not to learn of the Japanese surrender for many weeks. On 15 January, 1946, SOE ceased to exist. There was no place in peacetime for a highly secret organization steeped in sabotage and clandestine warfare. SOE had served its purpose, and served it well. The 'amateurs', who had provided by far and away the bulk of its strength, returned to their civilian occupation: bankers, stockbrokers, businessmen, academics, journalists, housewives, burglars, forgers, idealists, soldiers of fortune. A few could not face life without an edge to it.

MI6 was highly alert to the growing Soviet menace in Eastern Europe and indeed the world. There is no doubt it absorbed a number of individual SOE agents, men to whom the prospect of civilian life held few attractions after years of excitement. Len was not among those who went on to make a permanent career out of the Cold War, although, like those who did, he found the clamour for demobilization somewhat dispiriting.

It wasn't that he was sorry the war had ended; he had seen too much of its miseries for that. It was just that he was disinclined to join in the celebrations of peace. He was quite happy in his own mind that he had made the right decision to apply for a permanent commission; the country would still need an army in peacetime. It was just a question of being patient until things sorted themselves out and, secure in Connie's support, he faced the future with confidence. Belsen still disturbed his sleep, and he would occasionally wake up crying. But the human mind has an extraordinary capacity to pull down a shutter on unpleasant memories, and increasingly he withdrew into the cocoon of his small family. Despite shortages and rationing, a brave new postwar world was opening up — or so the politicians and papers said — and he had been accepted for a regular commission subject to attending an Officer Cadet Training Unit (OCTU).

Commissioned in the field, Len had not gone through the usual formalities of a War Office Selection Board, much less had any formal officer training. Now this had to be rectified. At OCTU Len took down his captain's stars and donned the white epaulette stripe and white backing to his capbadge, the insignia of an officer cadet. There were a few other wartime officers like him staying on, but he found little in common with them. The majority of the cadets were raw youngsters, cannon fodder for the expected war against Japan, kept on now to allow the longer serving men to be demobilized. As one who attended the same course has remarked, 'We couldn't fathom this "elderly" cadet with two rows of ribbons who kept himself to himself'.

His final report makes interesting reading. He was graded 'B' (above average) in all subjects except organization and administration where he got a 'D' (below average).[1] As Len says ruefully, 'There were not many socks to count where I had been.' But he agreed that the Commandant's assessment was 'pretty fair'.

> 'This officer is rather a lone wolf. This characteristic has been produced by his previous individualistic training. He has distinct ability in leadership. He must now apply himself to better his general education which is rather lacking.'

In January, 1946, he had his first taste of conventional soldiering since leaving the boys' company in Catterick in 1939, when he was posted as supernumerary signals officer to 15 Brigade Signal Squadron stationed at Wolfenbüttel on the border, close to what had become the Soviet zone of occupied Germany.

> 'It was peacetime all right. The Brigadier was a mad highlander who had brought out a pack of hounds, and blew his hunting horn when he wanted his orderly.'

Len's duties were far from onerous and, away from the bombed and shattered heartland of Germany, life was pleasant enough for the occupying troops. The *Reichsmark* was worthless and the British Armed Forces Vouchers (BAFVs), the currency issued to servicemen, could only be used in messes and the NAAFI. So the universal currency was the cigarette, with coffee or nylons as useful substitutes. Len, being an inveterate smoker, used most of his own ration himself but still managed to acquire the occasional present for Connie — a gold watch cost 100 cigarettes.

Fraternization with the Germans was forbidden, and such *bierkellers* (bars) or cafés that were open were out of bounds to the troops. Not that this prevented the ever-resourceful British soldier, and officer, from finding their 'bits of frat'. The German Army did not have officers' messes, so the headquarters mess was in a large house in the town, with the more junior officers billeted in another a few streets away. Returning to his room one evening shortly after his arrival, Len was greeted by the ample backside of one of the officers from the headquarters mess, where presumably there were less opportunities, busily engaged on top of one of the mess waitresses. Coughing politely, Len indicated that he would like to go to bed; it was, after all, his bed. He was told uncompromisingly to 'fuck off'.

'A jug of cold water soon cooled their ardour, but I don't know who was more embarrassed next morning when the same waitress served me my breakfast.'

Never one for social or mess life, Len indulged himself in the passion for reading he had acquired in Greece, and reverted to going for long solitary rambles in the countryside, keeping well back from the border, but watching with interest the British and Soviet armoured car patrols shadowing each other on either side of it. It was an interest which was to stand him in good stead in the months to come.

As he was under-employed, the Brigadier put him in charge of his kennels. It was the first time in his life that Len had had anything to do with dogs, but he enjoyed the foxhounds' boisterous affection when he made his rounds. It was not to last for long. One of the Alsatian guard dogs managed to get over the fence into the compound where the bitches on heat were kept. 'He was sitting there next morning with a bloody great grin on his face and his tongue lolling out.' It also struck Len that the Alsatian had a lot of satisfied customers.

'The Brigadier went berserk. I'd ruined his bloodline, and the bitches would never be any good again. He ranted and raved for half an hour.

The pups were a bloody funny-looking lot when they arrived, but even
the Brigadier saw the funny side eventually.'

Len, however, was soon to have another occupation. At a party in the mess
of a nearby cavalry regiment, a Lancer major took him aside.

'You're Willmott aren't you, ex-ISRB?'

'Yes', answered Len cautiously.

'Served in Greece, France and Holland?'

Len thought fast. He had told no one in the headquarters about his
wartime career. The Brigade Major had asked him about his decorations
when he joined, but he had replied noncommittally, just saying Greece and
France without elaboration. There were plenty of decorated officers around
in 1945 and, even with 'operational' parachute wings worn above them, his
medal ribbons usually went without comment. Did the Brigade Major know?
He could not be sure, but it was possible.

The Major continued, following Len's nod of assent.

'We have a small op running, perhaps you'd like to help. But we can't
talk here.'

It was a thoughtful Len who went back to his quarters that night. Here
was someone else who seemed to know all about him.

By arrangement, the Major joined Len on one of his walks the next
afternoon, guiding him rather closer to the border than he had been before.
They sat on a log in a clump of trees where they could see the border wire,
and lit cigarettes. The Major asked Len about the crossbred Alsatian/
Foxhound puppies, roaring with laughter at his description of what had
happened, particularly the Brigadier's reaction. It was all very relaxed and
friendly. Len reflected on how things had changed since pre-war that he
should be sitting chatting on equal terms with this casual 'toff' of a
cavalryman. Finally the Major got round to the subject he had broached the
night before.

There were some Germans living in the Soviet Zone whom the Allies
would prefer not to to fall into the hands of the communist authorities.
Would Len care to help bring them across the final mile or so into the British
Zone? There would be no more than three or four at a time, although some
might be women. He would explain in more detail later how it would be
done so as to avoid the Soviet patrols. 'It was all pretty straightforward
really.' Len would normally get twenty-four-hours' advance notice of when
he was needed. On no account must he mention this proposal to anyone; it
was a 'little sensitive'.

One can only assume that this was MI6 coming back into his life. It was
the start of the smuggling out of Eastern Europe of hundreds of people the
West wanted to make use of, or to deny their services to the Soviets.

Prominent scientists, especially those whose expertise was rocketry, were high on the priority list. This illicit trafficking in people, mostly East Germans, was to continue and expand throughout much of the Cold War. The CIA became heavily involved as well as MI6. It became highly dangerous and highly lucrative once the border was developed into a fortified zone with barbed wire, minefields, watch towers, and a permanent border guard force whose task was to kill escapees. A few individuals made substantial sums. At the time Len was approached it was still in its infancy, the whole operation less fraught and much simpler than it later became.

Characteristically Len asked no questions, saying merely that he would do what he could to help. He just assumed that his absences would be cleared with brigade headquarters.

His first operation came about a week later. The Major took him up to within sight of the border again and, with a map, pointed out the salient features — the border fence, a ditch beyond it, a couple of gates in a field, a village just under a mile into the Soviet Zone with a prominent church on which he should be able to navigate in the dark. Soviet armoured-car patrols always followed the British patrols on the opposite side of the border, something Len had noted from his earlier walks. He would go in one night and come out the next. He would be met at a rendezvous short of the village, and looked after until it was time to come out. It was only for the last few hundred yards that Len would be on his own. It all seemed straightforward.

So it was. The Major drove him down to a side road near the border just before dusk. The British armoured-car patrol came up the border road and, sure enough, shadowing them on the parallel track on the other side came the Soviets. The Major waited ten minutes and, as dusk settled, whispered to Len to be on his way. 'No, I wasn't frightened. I was never really in enemy territory, but the adrenalin was running. As the Major had said, "It was all pretty straightforward".'

Len slipped quickly through the wire, making for the ditch on the far side of the first field. There an English-speaking German awaited him who, after the initial whispered exchange, signalled Len to follow, leading him silently across the next field, through a gate through some woods to the outskirts of the village where he left Len while he went forward to check.

He spent the next day resting up in a German house in the village until his guide returned the following evening. He led him into the wood to meet his charges and Len was somewhat dismayed to find that two of the four were an elderly man and his wife. Then they went through the gate to the ditch where they crouched for the next hour. The elderly wife was weeping and whimpering so Len put a reassuring arm round her shoulders and whispered reassurance in her ear — 'Not that I think she understood a word, but the voice helped and she calmed down'.

As soon as the twin sets of lights of the British and Soviet patrols had passed the German tapped Len on the shoulder.

'It wasn't the old couple that caused the problem; they were great. It was the younger man who fell and twisted his ankle. He was about twice my size and I had to put his arm over my shoulder and hobble him the last couple of hundred yards. I had to tell him I'd hit him if he didn't shut up.'

They scrambled through the wire and, two hundred yards further on, arrived panting on the raised road. As promised, two cars were waiting, lights doused. The Major bundled the escapees into the first, patted Len on the shoulder with a very British 'Well done', and climbed in himself. A little deflated, Len got into the other car to be driven the few miles back to his unit.

'I only went over eight or nine times in the next five months. The pattern was always the same; I'd slip across at dusk one night, be met, taken to a house (not always the same one), next night I'd meet my "parcels", be led down to the last few hundred yards, through the wire, and up on to the road where the major would be waiting. There was nothing to it, really.'

But there was. There were only four 'parcels' the first time, as promised. On the second and subsequent trips Len never knew how many he would find at the rendezvous. On one occasion, expecting no more than four, there were over twenty, ranging from elderly women to small children. At this he baulked. He had taken ten out on an earlier occasion and he had been scared stiff and got a bollocking from the Major.

'It was a difficult decision deciding who I would take, and I had to give priority to the men who I assumed were the important parcels. But it was heart-rending.'

As with any operation Len, like most people, was apprehensive before he went in, although not to the same degree as when waiting inside an aircraft approaching a drop zone. Once over the wire he was mostly too busy to feel fear, although at twenty-five he was a lot more cautious than he was at the start of the war. He always had the utmost faith in the people looking after him. To Len they were the ones who made the decisions; he complied with orders, did his job, and never argued or queried aspects of the mission not within his area of responsibility. His comments on these smuggling expeditions and his job in Germany were prosaic — 'It didn't take up much time. The rest was routine signals duties and, to begin with, the kennels, then, after the Brigadier forgave me, the kennels again.'

The summer of 1946 saw Len's first posting to a conventional peacetime signals job. He was the second-in-command of 13 Brigade Signals squadron, based in Trieste. Although delighted to be accompanied by Connie, who was then expecting their second child, a son, he was not much inspired by his duties. Like the second-in-command of most things his work was basically administrative, 'counting socks and accounts,' as he put it.

The only incident of that period that he recalled with interest was the meeting with his old former company commander from Catterick days, Colonel Boileau, who was then the Commander Royal Signals in Trieste. 'He hadn't changed much; still a cold, aloof bastard, and I'm not sure he even recognized me until I reminded him.' This is possibly unfair to Tommy Boileau who did indeed recognize him and remembered Len as 'a very ordinary boy, but a bit of a scallywag'.[2] To find him as a much bemedalled captain was something of a surprise.

It so happened that Boileau's and Len's tours ended at the same time. Len had discovered, along with many others, that Mussolini had cornered the fur market in his brief but inglorious reign. As a result furs could be picked up for a pittance on the black market. Len had acquired a 'nice bit of rabbit' for Connie. She was all for wearing it on the way home, but Len demurred. Instead he had it sewn into his army mac as a winter lining. In the mess the night before their departure he heard Boileau recounting how he had bought a mink coat for his wife. Never holding a grudge, Len suggested quietly that the Colonel did what everybody else was doing and have it sewn into the lining of his coat. Boileau thanked him and went off to arrange it.

At the Customs in Dover Len opened up his coat and said, 'Winter lining — rabbit'. The Customs Officer smiled knowingly and passed him through. A few paces behind him he heard the same officer say to Boileau, 'Rabbit?' and his indignant response, 'No it bloody well isn't, it's mink.' 'The last I saw of Boileau was he was being led aside and getting out his chequebook.'

When Len had applied for his regular commission he had recorded in the appropriate box that he spoke Greek. He thought it might help his application. The authorities responsible for postings in the British Army are not noted for putting round pegs in round holes, but, reporting back after his leave, Len found a posting order awaiting him as a liaison officer to the Greek forces in the British Military Mission in Athens. It was a time of great turmoil and bloodshed in that country, where the third and most savage of the communist uprisings had erupted. Nevertheless, it was a married accompanied tour so Len was delighted to be taking his young family to the country from which he had sent his coded marriage proposal.

Allotted a summer villa in the hills around Athens, Connie rapidly turned it into a home, while Len travelled extensively on his liaison duties. One pleasurable task was to call on General Napoleon Zervas, the wartime EDES *andarte* leader with whom he had spent so many months in the mountains. Zervas, now Minister of Public Order, greeted him with a bearhug and loud shouts for *ouzo*.

Their house was beautiful in warm weather, but bitter in winter. The winter of 1947 was a particularly hard one and the Greek Army, which was supposed to provide wood for their stove and heating, just did not deliver. After repeated requests Len took matters into his own hands and, as he had done during the war, cut down the nearest olive tree. For this arbitrary action they found themselves in the midst of an unpleasant international incident. Olive trees in Greece have a multiplicity of owners. All were enraged. With Len away so much, Connie bore the brunt of the consequences. Then anonymous telephone calls started. At first she thought they were just nuisance calls; silence and heavy breathing when she picked up the receiver. Next came messages like: 'Your husband has had an accident,' or 'Your husband will have an accident if he goes out tomorrow'. These were followed by more direct threats, in which Len was called a Fascist pig and the children were threatened with kidnapping. 'To begin with I didn't tell Len because I thought it was the locals trying to get their own back for cutting down the tree, but then I became more frightened.' Len had been on the Communist death list in 1944. It seemed they had long memories. Threats to himself did not worry him, but those to his family were an entirely different matter. The British Military Mission were sceptical, the inference being that Connie was exaggerating, but in any case there was little they could do. Never one to take officialdom or the proper channels too seriously, Len went direct to Zervas and told him, in Greek, exactly what he faced. By nightfall a dozen para-military gendarmes were pitching their tents in his garden. Connie was embarrassed by the fuss she had caused but 'they were nice lads and wonderful with the children'. The telephone calls never recurred.

Len's contribution to British-Greek relations is hard to evaluate as it was, for the most part, at low level. In his own words he was little more than 'a fetcher and carrier of messages — a courier'. He moved extensively through operational areas where there was always the element of risk. His command of colloquial Greek, and his ability to interpret British advice and suggestions in the face of growing Greek disillusionment with Britain's power to influence matters, was undoubtedly an asset. Perhaps too, his knack of being able to have a glass or two of *ouzo* with Greek staff officers and junior commanders, swopping stories with them in Greek, gave him an influence beyond his rank and status.

Len's three years in Greece passed soon enough. He had enjoyed them and felt confident that he had made a worthwhile contribution. Captain Demetrious, an English-speaking Greek in the liaison team, had nothing but praise for Len's small but important part in the complex political situation at that time. He wrote: 'Len was special. He knew and understood the Greeks; they would listen to him. We were extremely sorry when he left.'[3]

From Greece Len was sent to Tripoli, an eventful move with threats to bomb the ship in Piraeus harbour, plus a stormy passage from Malta. There followed a year in which Connie soaked up the sun, strolled in the *souk*, and generally relaxed, enjoying the life of a divisional headquarters at a time when the British Army still lived well in overseas garrisons. Apart from several months in the Canal Zone in Egypt, when Britain intervened there in 1951, it was an uneventful posting for Len.

Back in Britain after five years overseas, Len had every right to expect a home posting but, seemingly, somebody somewhere remembered his background. For the umpteenth time he was invited to the War Office. The newly re-formed SAS needed a signals officer. Would he like the job?

CHAPTER TEN

THE SAS AGAIN

'The signals were a shambles, but it was more the fault of the kit than the blokes, although training was poor. The signallers got little support from patrol commanders and had no confidence in themselves or their sets.'

It is undisputed that the resurrection of the regular SAS in Malaya in 1950 got off to a thoroughly bad start. The many ill-disciplined, scruffy and hard-drinking members who were recruited into the Malayan Scouts gave the SAS a disreputable reputation that was to last for many years among more conventional soldiers, including many in high places. Today its fame for excellence is universal; it is expected to, and frequently does, achieve military miracles. The word 'élite' is anathema to the SAS, but today in their field they admit few equals. When Len joined them over forty years ago in Malaya, their reputation was at its nadir.

The original SAS Brigade had been disbanded in October, 1945. The rash of irregular units born during the war was quickly killed off in peace, their officers and men dispersed to regular units to await discharge or absorption into the peacetime Army. The British military establishment has always had an in-built distrust for special forces. It is a prejudice among many professional soldiers which exists even today, when the skills and qualities of the SAS are much more in the public eyes than they have ever been. That is part of the problem; there is the element of envy present.

A few farsighted individuals — notably David Stirling himself, Paddy Mayne, who had commanded 1 SAS, Brian Franks, who had commanded 2 SAS and others — felt passionately that the standards of excellence and expertise forged in war behind enemy lines should not be lost to the British Army. General Browning had told the Regiment near the end of the war in Germany:

'The operations you have carried out have had more effect in hastening the disintegration of the German Army than any other single effort. . . . You have done a job of work which . . . no other troops in the world could have done.'[1]

After a protracted battle with the War Office, including much lobbying at the top, agreement was eventually given for the formation of a Territorial SAS Regiment. With typical SAS logic it was decided that it would be invidious to call the new regiment 1st or 2nd SAS; 12 SAS did not sound right so, based on the old Artists Rifles, the 1 and 2 were reversed and the 21st Special Air Service Regiment (Artists) was created in February, 1947, under Brian Franks' command. Franks was also the managing director of the Hyde Park Hotel Group. Both institutions flourished, and still do.

In 1948 the Malayan Emergency burst on an unprepared British Army. By 1950 communist insurgents, the majority from the predominantly communist Malayan Peoples' Anti-Japanese Army, had inflicted substantial casualties: 863 civilians, 323 police officers and 154 soldiers.[2] Road travel was risky except with an armed convoy, and the CTs (Communist Terrorists) had seriously disrupted the all-important rubber and tin industries.

The task of creating a special military force to take on the terrorists at their own game, living deep in the jungle for weeks or months at a time, was given to a tough, hard-fighting, hard-drinking sapper officer called Calvert, then on the staff in Hong Kong. Calvert, who had earned a double Blue at Oxford, had gained the soubriquet 'Mad Mike' for some of his less conventional activities. During the war he had had a distinguished, if unusual, career in the Burmese jungle both as a Column Commander and Brigade Commander in Orde Wingate's Chindits. He had also commanded the SAS Brigade in North-West Europe for the last ten months of the war.

The first squadron, A Squadron, was a very mixed bag, including many of whom regular battalions were only too glad to see the back; the hard cases, many of whom had seen substantial service in military detention barracks — even ten deserters from the French Foreign Legion — were taken without hesitation. There was also good material. Veterans from SOE, the original SAS, Force 136 and Ferret Force, men with outstanding war records like Len's, responded. Among them were two officers who were to be the architects of the SAS as they are known today. The lean, thoughtful brewer's son from Devon, John Woodhouse who, as SAS legend has it, lived on a tin of sardines a day, and a bespectacled Suffolk clergyman's son, Dare Newell, who had seen service behind enemy lines with SOE in Albania and Malaya. It was the latter who was subsequently to be known by the affectionate and well-deserved nickname of Godfather to the SAS.

Shortly afterwards a second squadron, B Squadron, arrived from England, drawn from TA volunteers of the reconstituted 21 SAS. Most had served in the wartime SAS but none had any experience of jungle warfare. To complete the Regiment, C (Rhodesian) Squadron, selected from over 1,000 volunteers, arrived from Africa — large, tough, bronzed men with an abundance of bush experience, but little affinity with the Malaysian natives.

A Squadron quickly made a name for themselves for drunkenness, indiscipline and wild behaviour. Nor was their operational record particularly good, although one patrol stayed in the jungle for 103 days, a feat that no infantry battalion, including Gurkhas, had accomplished. Their kill-to-contact ratio was lower than most, while their contact-to-patrol-days ratio was lower still. Stories were rife of wild parties culminating in competitions where drunken officers competed with drunken sergeants to see who could get the largest number of 3-inch mortar bombs in the air before the first one landed, and other dangerous excesses. They were stories which doubtless grew in the telling but contained more than an element of truth.

Their role was totally different to the normal infantry battalion — long penetration patrols, bolstering the shy and primitive Sakai tribes, and by their very presence in deep jungle keeping the terrorists on the move. However, the regular British and Gurkha battalions were unimpressed. B Squadron from England, and C Squadron from Rhodesia when it arrived, were not impressed either. When the name of the Regiment was changed to 22nd Special Air Service, the reputation of A Squadron stuck and critics of the SAS lumped the whole Regiment together. Sadly too, there were incidents in the two new squadrons which upset Stirling when they were reported to him. This bad reputation was to take many years to live down. The antics and the excesses of the SAS were widely discussed by young officers serving in regular units or on the staff in Malaya. Some of them were to rise to high rank in the Army, with their view of the SAS coloured twenty and more years later by what they knew directly or by hearsay of 22 SAS in Malaya.

Much credit is due to Calvert for his concept of operations, and in creating the Regiment, but his name is inevitably associated in SAS eyes with the inauspicious beginnings of 22 SAS, together with the many problems that flowed from it in the years to come. Calvert's administrative difficulties with his widely scattered Regiment were enormous and were aggravated by his personal refusal to doff his cap to authority. This was part of the reason that he never really won the confidence and backing of his superior headquarters.

His large, imperturbable Adjutant, Pat Winter, an officer who found it hard to fit into the ceremonial routine of the peacetime Scots Guards, did his best to protect his Commanding Officer from himself. Calvert had recruited him in an aeroplane from Hong Kong at the height of an electrical storm. As Winter has said, when Calvert disliked some administrative problem his solution was usually to 'collect half a dozen of the blokes and disappear into the *ulu* [jungle] for a couple of weeks'.[3] By the middle of 1951 Calvert had shot his bolt. He was a sick man. He had driven himself mercilessly for twelve years, even his champion boxer and front row forward physique, plus his obsessive determination to keep going, was finally defeated. He was invalided back to England suffering from malaria, dysentery, hookworm and the general depredations of extreme climates.

He was replaced by a burly, 6'4" Highlander called John Sloane who had no experience whatever of special forces or irregular warfare. His task was to sort out this unruly, far from popular, fledgling regiment. Early in his tenure of command he sent one of his squadron commanders, John Woodhouse, at Woodhouse's instigation, back to England to establish a recruiting and selection system more in keeping with SAS principles. It was a move that laid the foundations of the present-day rigorous procedure.

It was at this point that the quiet, self-effacing new Signals Officer arrived. He had given his new job much thought on the long, uncomfortable journey out on a converted Lancaster bomber. He was returning at last to where he believed he belonged. On the train from Singapore to the then SAS base at Kluang in Johore he gazed with interest at the matted undergrowth, towering trees that flanked the railway track which gave fleeting glimpses of the jungle canopy stretching interminably to the horizon on either side.

At Kluang station there was no one to meet him. Len frowned to himself, remembering the cheerful young officer who had met the equally young sergeant at Kabrit ten years before. He thought it strange, but perhaps his signal had not got through. Clearly, from what he had seen, communications in this sort of environment were probably difficult. After some prudent negotiations he found a taxi to take him to the SAS camp.

His arrival appalled him. Irregular soldier though he was, his first impression came as a shock. The sentry at the gate was smoking and failed to salute. Len asked the way to the Officers' Mess, only to be given grudging, surly directions. Perhaps he was asking too much, but in reality he knew from the moment he entered the camp that things were wrong, although he was unaware of the origins of the Malayan Scouts, or what had gone before during the last few hectic months. There was a noisy alcoholic party going on in the Mess, so he sought out the Mess Sergeant and got himself installed in a tent. It had been a strangely disappointing day, not just because he had not found what he expected, but because he could not reconcile what he had found in Malaya with what he had seen of the original SAS in Egypt in 1941.

The next morning Len reported to the Adjutant, as required of all newly arrived officers. He remembers Winter as large, welcoming, a bit distant, and preoccupied. Winter was indeed preoccupied. Loyal as he was to Calvert, he knew that things were very wrong. The Regiment's communications were a shambles and Len's predecessor had earned himself the nickname 'Spanner'; if it were possible for anything to go wrong 'Spanner' made certain that it did. Central to the problem in 1952 was that no one seriously expected the wireless to work in the jungle. If patrols or outstations managed to get through it was a bonus.[4]

Communications were only one of the Adjutant's worries. His principal preoccupation was translating into practical form Sloane's efforts to transform a rabble into some sort of military order. The quiet new Signal Officer made little impression on him at the time, apart from the fact that he was polite, well turned out, and did not add to his problems.[5]

Len first drew attention to himself over the matter of drill parades or, more precisely, the Signals Officer's absence from the first Adjutant's Parade. Drill as a panacea of all evils is deeply ingrained in any guardsman's soul and, as part of the Sloane sorting-out process, Winter had ordered a series of RSM's and Adjutant's drill parades. They were a disaster. On the first RSM's parade B Squadron did not show up at all.

On the Adjutant's parade there was a distinct shortage of officers, and, in the middle of it, the Rhodesian Squadron decided it was not for them, turned smartly to their right and marched off. Winter vented his rage on the officers who had failed to parade, only to be told politely but firmly by Len that, counting his Other Rank service as half (as he was entitled to do), he was in fact the senior of the two. As the orders had only specified officers junior to the Adjutant, he had not paraded. He detected a glint of amusement in the small man's clear gaze as Len added, 'Perhaps drill parades are not what's needed to knock this lot into shape'. A roar of laughter erupted from Winter's vast frame. RSM's and Adjutant's parades passed into history.

Len set about learning and solving the complications of signalling in Malaya. Conditions for good wireless reception could hardly have been worse. Mountains, trees and atmospherics combined to make clear communications the remote exception rather than the rule. During the monsoon, for example, there were daily thunderstorms with continuous flashes of lightning and thunder lasting up to an hour.

Then there were difficulties with the wireless itself. The main patrol set was a tropicalised version of the pre-war 18 set. It was bulky, burdensome, and many signallers of that day believed that the best way of tuning the transmitter to a recalcitrant receiver was to kick it. It also required a heavy dry battery, the useful life of which was short and unpredictable. SAS patrols, deep in the jungle for weeks and months on end, had either to have a regular supply of new batteries by air, thus compromising their whereabouts, or take in the even larger 62 set designed for vehicles. It was not the weight of the set so much as having to take accumulator batteries with a pedal generating machine to recharge them.

The British strategic plan to deny the jungle terrorists food, a product of Calvert's fertile mind, was beginning to take effect, driving the CTs further and further into the jungle, many miles from habitation, thus forcing them to clear areas of jungle to grow food. These were easily spotted from the air.

Shortly after Len's arrival plans were made to attack a complex of CT gardens in the far North of Malaya near the Thai border; it was called the Belum Valley operation. To achieve surprise, the SAS decided that one squadron would parachute in. The distances and terrain gave the Signals Officer formidable communications problems, but it was the concept of jumping into the jungle (tree jumping) that was the real unknown, especially for the operators jumping with the cumbersome sets. The theory was simple. You selected a suitable tree as you approached the jungle canopy, praying your parachute would snag in the upper branches. A hundred feet of rope was provided for each man with which to abseil to the ground. In practice it was more as described by Major John Salmon, the second-in-command of 22 SAS:

'Next thing you know you are floating through the air, and it's one of the most wonderful feelings in the world; then you see the trees coming. You are coming down beautifully, steering for the middle of the trees. The hot air makes you swing violently, as if a giant had caught hold of you. You let the air spill out of the chute and look for a good, healthy tree. Sometimes you make that spot; often you don't. It's hard to tell until you are a few feet away. When you hit a tree you don't know whether you will stay there or not. Often the branch snaps so you hurtle down, smashing into the branches on the way, until you finally come to a halt. If it holds, then you know you are safe.'[6]

Although there were no casualties on the Belum Valley operation and tree jumping became an SAS speciality, it soon came to be regarded for what it was, a dangerous way to descend. Casualties mounted, including one horrific occasion when an NCO, in agony with his harness twisted round his private parts, cut himself free and dropped 150 feet to his death.

Without fuss Len set about putting the signals right with the help of the vastly experienced Sergeant Steve Stevenson.[7] Slowly, Winter began to take note of this quiet, almost shy officer. The standard of communications improved dramatically, even though, as is the lot of all signals officers, they get precious little credit for it, and plenty of brickbats when the wireless does not work. Len remained unobtrusive, but if there was a signals breakdown in one of the jungle forts Len got there somehow to put it right. He was indefatigable in getting new and better wireless sets, repairing existing ones, and going to endless trouble to train the operators to give them confidence in their equipment. He could also be demanding, requiring reasons in writing if a patrol was out of communication for more than forty-eight hours.

Dare Newell, then a sabre squadron commander, also noted the improvements. He had heard about Len Willmott while he was in Albania, and it was he who had suggested that Len might make a suitable signals officer for 22 SAS. He was to comment many years later, 'Len was the best bloody signals officer we ever had, and SAS communications would have been much better, much sooner, had he stayed with us longer.'[8]

Dare Newell was transferred to Headquarters Squadron to put the Regiment's administration on a proper footing and take over responsibility for in-theatre recruitment and training. So the long haul back to SAS standards got under way. Coincidentally Len came directly under Dare's command, and the job of MTO (Motor Transport Officer) fell vacant.

There was no replacement immediately available so Len acquired the job in addition to his own. The traffic-accident returns dropped markedly, and officers found it increasingly difficult to get hold of jeeps for private purposes. As usual Len always seemed to be about when needed; if there was a driver short Len would drive the ration lorry or the water truck; if a patrol was due out of the jungle on to a road that ran through a 'black' (terrorist-dominated) area Len invariably took the convoy out himself.[9]

The Adjutant's first real clash with Len came over a Court Martial. A Rhodesian trooper had refused a parachute jump — a court-martial offence in any airborne unit. The trooper was entitled by law to — and needed — a defending officer. He was also one of the Rhodesian Squadron signallers so he asked for Len to defend him because 'he looked after his blokes'.

'Bloody man, Len,' said Winter years later; 'He went through the SOPs (Standard Operational Procedures) with a fine toothcomb and found one discrepancy in them. I'd presented an open-and-shut case as Prosecuting Officer, and bloody Willmott got up and said there was "No case to answer".'[10] The Rhodesian got off. Winter was glad he did in retrospect as he redeemed himself later. Winter apart, the Rhodesian Squadron Commander, Peter Wall, afterwards to become a Lieutenant-General and Chief of the Defence Staff in the Rhodesian Armed Forces, was furious.

Life in 22 SAS continued to be eventful. Colonel Sloane was relieved in mid-1953 by Lieutenant-Colonel Oliver Brooke of the Manchester Regiment, another Regular soldier with no experience of special forces but very different from Sloane. Brooke was a fierce, quick-tempered extrovert, more than a match for the still intractable members of the SAS. The evening before he was due to assume command a group of NCOs and men, who had imbibed not too wisely in the town, decided to wake up the new Commanding Officer. They let off an explosive charge outside the Officers' Mess, the destructive effect of which they clearly underestimated. It blew down the wall. The table next to which Brooke was standing took off and landed about twenty feet away. Dare Newell was standing next to Brooke and the outgoing Commanding Officer, Sloane, while Len was sitting in a corner sipping a beer.

'I hit the deck like everyone else but, bugger me, there were Brooke, Sloane and Dare still standing and chatting away as if nothing had happened.'

Next day, a Sunday, Brooke took over command officially. Within a couple of hours he had sacked sixteen NCOs and troopers. They were out of camp an hour later. This was what the SAS needed. Unfortunately it was not to last long. Brooke suffered appalling injuries on a tree jump and was flown home to England to spend many months in hospital.

Not long afterwards Dare Newell was posted back to England to set up the first SAS staff representation in the War Office, a single grade III staff officer. It was the only staff representation the SAS was to have for many years. Len was promoted Acting Major and took over Headquarter Squadron with responsibility for administration, signals, transport, supplies and, most important, in-theatre selection and training. He had come a long way from being a boy wireless operator.

As Winter said, 'You hardly noticed Len. HQ Squadron just ran, and he was always around when needed.'[11] It was a job Len relished. He had been well trained and briefed by Newell and he could put into practice many of the things he had learned from the New Zealanders in Greece, and had thought about ever since his first exposure to the SAS in Kabrit ten or more years earlier.

Newell undoubtedly knew something about Len's SOE background and his wartime career, but Winter had not the slightest idea that he had a distinguished SOE record behind him until 1989. 'I took him as a good but straight-up-and-down signal officer. He never spoke of the war.' Johnny Cooper, one of Stirling's originals and his driver and gunner in the desert (now Lieutenant-Colonel John Cooper MBE DCM MM), was MTO when Len arrived, and a sabre squadron commander for the rest of Len's tour, had no idea either.[12] Both served with Len for two years in Malaya. To 22 SAS in Malaya he was just 'a quiet little bloke who did a good job'.

With the SAS taking shape according to Stirling's principles, and the gradual weeding out of undesirable and unsuitable officers and men, Len really felt he was back where he belonged. The quality of recruits arriving in Malaya from John Woodhouse's embryo organization in England was improving with each intake. High-quality young officers were arriving, including such more recent SAS 'greats' as Captain the Hon John Slim (now Colonel the Viscount Slim OBE), Captain Johnny Watts (now Lieutenant-General Sir John Watts, KBE, MC and bar) and 'DLB' (now General Sir Peter de la Billière, KCB, KBE, DSO, MC and bar), all of whom were eventually to command 22 SAS. The morale of the Regiment soared. Life looked set fair for Major Len Willmott, MM, BEM.

Then disaster struck. Connie nearly died giving birth to their third child. The baby was badly scarred and both were evacuated to England by air as the only way of saving mother and daughter. Len, desperately worried at the prospect of losing his precious Connie, agonized for several days. Until now the Army had always come first, before any family or personal considerations. He was torn by a terrible dilemma. It was the Adjutant who resolved his problem. 'I just told him that this was one occasion when his family came first, so he was to fly home.' Although he did not know it, this was the end of Len's special forces career.

Toward the end of the 1950s Newell, as the SAS representative in the War Office, moved heaven and earth to get Len back to 22 SAS for their first tour in the Oman — the Jebel Akhdar campaign. For once he failed. Acting Major Willmott had not passed his captain-to-major promotion examination so his future retention was under review.

Perhaps the attitude of a grateful government can be summed up in a reply from the War Office to an enquiry from the New Zealand High Commission at the time Len was recruited into the New Zealand Security Service. It is dated Stanmore, 5 May, 1970. The first paragraph lists the dates of his service in the ranks, both boy service and man service. The second paragraph lists his promotions and relinquishments as an officer. The third paragraph states baldly:

Awarded the British Empire Medal, London Gazette — 12 Oct 43
Awarded the Military Medal, London Gazette — 4 Feb 44
Awarded the French *Croix de Guerre* and the Bronze Lion of the Netherlands.
Served overseas.

The final paragraph reads:

This officer failed to pass his the Captain to Major promotion examination, otherwise his service has been 'satisfactory'.[13] The italics are mine.

EPILOGUE

'I have a message from Colonel Smirnoff [KGB Resident in New Zealand]. He is sorry that Mr Willmott was not there to see him off. He had hoped to shake your hand.'

Connie watched Len's face with growing apprehension as he opened and read the official letter. He looked at her with misery in his eyes. The letter left no room for doubt. Beyond the perfunctory thanks there was only one sentence that mattered; 'Your services are no longer required'. Len was shattered. He had been in the Army since he was fifteen; he was now almost forty-one with a wife and three children, no home of his own, few qualifications for civilian life, minimal savings, and Britain in the throes of a severe economic downturn. Despite all the vicissitudes that he had weathered cheerfully in the past, Len sank into the hopeless inactivity that comes with deep depression. Connie bore the brunt of it. It was she who eventually pulled him round. 'Len was like a lost soul; the Army had always moved us before. He didn't even know how to get hold of packing cases.'

The correspondence leading up to the half-anticipated bombshell had been protracted, just long enough for Len to complete twenty years reckonable service, and thus qualify for the minimum pension of £607 per annum. The problem was that Len had failed to pass his captain-to-major promotion exam, and the Army was overloaded with wartime officers who had elected to stay on. The slimming-down exercise had started in earnest and Len, however distinguished his career, was just one of many casualties. Britain is not always good at looking after those who have served her selflessly without thought for the morrow.

The papers in his personal file tell the story; the generals were sympathetic but civil servants made the rules and stuck to them. The file does not make happy reading. The armed services are a young man's profession — Len, as a forty-year-old temporary major who had failed to qualify for substantive promotion, was perhaps inevitably among the first to go.

Now he can look back on it as one of the milestones of his life. At the time it was traumatic to face a civilian future after twenty-six years in uniform. He was then the Second-in-Command and Training Major of the Royal

Signals Junior Leaders Regiment at Newton Abbot in Devonshire. It was a job he enjoyed. It took him back to his own beginnings; boys from not dissimilar backgrounds to his own joining at fifteen, and he was able to give them all the benefit of his own experience. He found it easy to relate to the young. For Connie it had been a happy and contented period with Len home every night and no sudden or unexplained disappearances. Len's posting to Newton Abbot had been the first real stability she had known. It had taken even her robust constitution a long time to get back to full health after the birth of their third child, Penny, who had had to undergo twenty-three operations to repair the damage of her birth. That period of stability had been much needed. Now everything was in the melting pot.

Len was depressed about Britain too, seeing little future for himself as a civilian. It was Connie who suggested, 'Well, you're always talking about those New Zealanders in the war; what about going to New Zealand?'

Len looked at his wife in amazement and his old decisiveness flooded back. The next morning he set off for New Zealand House in London, where he was interviewed by the Defence Attaché who got him to complete an application to join the New Zealand Army. He returned home beaming.

The weeks dragged by with nothing from the New Zealand High Commission. Enquiries at New Zealand House all produced the same response; the Defence Attaché was away on long leave, and they were still waiting to hear from Wellington. Len's slender finances were dwindling rapidly. He made his decision and headed for the P&O shipping offices.

By splitting up the family, sharing with others, and accepting the cheapest berths going, Len calculated he could just afford it by commuting half his pension, selling his car and all but a few precious bits of furniture. Six weeks later the family embarked on the SS *Ranjituri* for Wellington and a new life. He had no accommodation booked at the other end, no job, and precious little left of his savings. He did not even tell his brother, already in New Zealand, the date they were arriving. Len was off into unknown territory again, the adrenalin was running and he was supremely confident it would work out.

They arrived in Wellington on 11 May, 1962. Len got a taxi and asked to be taken to a hotel — any hotel. The taxi driver scratched his head and, with New Zealand directness asked, 'How much you got to spend, mate?' Len said he was not bothered as long as it had beds and a meal.

Next morning he located Army HQ to ask for an interview. A New Zealand Brigadier greeted him with surprise. Army headquarters had been chasing London for weeks to find out what had happened to Len as they were prepared to offer him a commision plus an assisted passage. Now the options were a Lieutenant's commission in the New Zealand Signals or a civilian appointment with the equivalent rank of Captain in Army Security.

Len opted for the latter, asked for a week to get his family settled, and returned to his hotel rejoicing. There was no suggestion, however, that the cost of his passages should be refunded.

Then he 'phoned his brother, a County Clerk in the far NW of North Island. Brother John, who appears to have been as decisive as Len, booked the family by plane to Gisborne, met them there and drove the family the twenty or thirty miles to his base at Tolega Bay. Connie had never had a car drive like it. John 'drove like a maniac, talking all the time', and the road twisted and turned through the spectacular northern range of mountains, with precipitous drops within a few feet of the narrow laterite track. Connie shut her eyes.

The township of Tolega Bay had her gasping with astonishment. 'It was like the Wild West — just one street about 100 yards wide, with a shop at one end and a pub at the other.' She thought it was grand. They had arrived on a Saturday — cinema night in the local woolshed. The children jumped up and down with excitement, begging to be allowed to go. Connie looked with some apprehension as horseman after horseman cantered up the street, jumped off his mount and tied it to a hitching-rail outside the pub. Most were wiry, powerfully-built brown men — Connie had never seen a Maori — and it was not long before the noise from the pub was deafening.

John Willmott roared with laughter at Connie's fears, and told her the Maoris were as gentle as kittens with children for all their wild warlike looks. Sharp at 6 p.m. the pub closed and the horsemen, each carrying a saddle and a flagon of beer, made for the cinema and, ignoring the benches, settled themselves against their saddles to watch the movie with rapt attention. The film over, they saddled up and rode out of town, some for distances of thirty miles. Connie decided she was going to like New Zealand.

Len returned to Wellington and rented a house for the family. His eldest daughter got a job in the security registry. Everything was working out. It was not long before Len got a mortgage, and they settled into a home of their own, the first of two they were to own.

Len threw himself into his new job with his usual quiet enthusiasm, finding that he had more than enough on his plate. In his view the New Zealand Army was the most un-security-conscious organization he had ever encountered. There was no key control, and the safes were antediluvian: 'You could have opened most of them with a tin opener.'

The occasion which he remembers best was being sent to have a look at the Government House safe. The Governor General of the day was that redoubtable soldier and author, Brigadier The Lord Ballantrae (Bernard Fergusson of Chindit fame). Len was ushered into his study in some trepidation — apart from anything else, it was the first 'lord' he had ever encountered. The Governor General screwed his monocle into his eye to glare at Len over a bushy moustache. Len stood to attention in his civvy suit.

'It's quite genuine, y'know,' he barked. 'Other eye's perfectly good, but half-blind in this one.'

'Yes, Sir,' acknowledged Len.

'Had a bunch of Kiwis during the war who paraded the next morning, every man jack wearing a penny in one eye, so I flipped me monocle into the air and caught in me eye,' he added, expertly doing just that — a well know Bernard Fergusson trick.

Len contributed another polite, 'Yes Sir.'

'Then I said, "Do that you bastards," and walked off parade. No more trouble with that lot.' He finished with an impish grin.

There was a pause as the great man surveyed Len though his monocle. The countless officers and men, and people from all walks of life, who knew, respected and loved Bernard Fergusson would be familiar with his staccato style of speech which belied his intense interest in people, and his quite extraordinary capacity for kindness.

'So you're Willmott,' he said eventually, 'but you're not a Kiwi.'

'No, I mean yes Sir,' stammered Len, now thoroughly confused.

'Well, come and sit down and tell me about yourself,' were Ballantrae's next words, 'What were you?'

'Royal Signals,' said Len.

'Ye must ha' been more than that. The chit here says you are Major Willmott MM BEM and you've got a couple of foreign gongs as well. Where d'ye get them?'

'Greece, Brittany and Holland,' said Len, 'but about your safe, Sir.'

'Ah, that's what you've come for. I suppose you'll have to tell me about your war another time — sounds interesting.' With that his lordship proceded to rummage in the top drawer of his desk until he produced an enormous key for a safe that Len reckoned must have arrived with the first Governor.

'You shouldn't really keep your safe-key in the drawer of your desk, Sir.'

'Only sensible place,' was the retort; 'Otherwise I'd never find the bloody thing.'

'Might I have a look inside, Sir?' The safe contained Lady Ballantrae's jewellery and a half-dozen bottles of malt whisky. Len felt he was rapidly losing control of the situation, and it was all he could do to stop bursting out laughing.

'And your secret and confidential papers, Sir?'

'Where I can find them,' said the Governor General; 'Right here in the bottom drawer. Don't worry; I've got another key.' He resumed his rummaging in his top drawer. Glancing up, he caught the look of utter incredulity on Len's face, glared at him for a second, then burst out into roars of laughter. 'Bloody man,' he said wiping his monocle, 'Look, we better have a dram and talk over what you want. Like the malt? Only place to keep it from the ADCs is in the safe.'

It was, Len says, one of the more remarkable interviews in his career, but 'What a bloody wonderful man'. There are many who would echo that sentiment.

Connie had settled in quickly, but, with the eldest daughter working and the younger children at school, found time on her hands. She had, after all, worked all her life. That problem was solved by Shirley. She came home one day full of glee at being promoted. Looking at her mother, she added, 'Why don't you apply for my job in the registry, Mum?'

So a team of three Willmotts found themselves working for Army Security. It was all highly satisfactory. In due course Connie became Chief Filing Clerk, and remained so for the next sixteen years. In New Zealand eyes she was better than any computer. 'Connie could find any file and any reference in a matter of minutes. We were lost for weeks after she finally left.'

There were to be two other phases in Len's seventeen-year career in New Zealand. In 1970 he was invited to transfer to the New Zealand equivalent of MI5. His four years there are still too recent for him to talk about. All he will say about his activities is that he was only a leg man, his main job being keeping an eye on the Soviet Defence Attaché, the KGB Resident in New Zealand, 'Colonel Smirnoff'.

One evening there was an urgent telephone call to the effect that Colonel Smirnoff had crossed the ferry to Picton on South Island in a civilian car. Len raced to Wellington Airport and caught a plane to Christchurch to pick up an unmarked car on the other side. The District Officer on South Island told him that Smirnoff had travelled south from Picton in the direction of Dunedin.

A wild drive through the night followed with police patrols radioing Smirnoff's progress and whereabouts. Telling the police not to stop the Colonel on any account, Len and the District Officer picked up the trail and were taken on a hair-raising wild-goose chase round country roads and into the mountains. Clearly the Colonel knew he had a tail, and was hell-bent on losing it. It says something for Len's driving that they stayed with him; it was in fact the first time he had put his comprehensive pre-war driver training fully to the test. Finally the Colonel slowed and drove back to Picton without completing whatever mission he had set out upon and booked onto the early morning ferry to Wellington.

Len caught the same ferry, noting with satisfaction the wisps of steam emanating from the Colonel's car. Catching sight of Len, Colonel Smirnoff — or whatever his real name was — treated him to a wintry smile. Len smiled back and bowed courteously. He had, after all, rather enjoyed the chase.

Len remembers the Colonel with some affection, feeling that he had got to know him rather well, 'And he did have a sense of humour'. When the Colonel finally left New Zealand, Len had returned to the Defence Department. The telephone rang in his office. It was the airport manager at Wellington airport, an old friend of Len's from his Security Service days: 'I have a message from Colonel Smirnoff. He is sorry that Mr Willmott was not there to see him off. He had hoped to shake your hand!'

Four years of broken nights and being called out at all hours had begun to pall. Connie, although she never commented or complained, was more than relieved at Len's return to the Defence Department with its more civilised working hours. She knew, as did Len, that his promotion prospects in the Security Service were strictly limited. Until now the post of Director of Civil Defence had always been reserved for the retiring Chief of Army Staff (CGS), but out of the blue the General asked Len to join him as his deputy.

It was a good job, carrying both a double promotion in the Civil Service and a substantial increase in pay, and 'it was interesting if not unduly exacting'. They settled down to a life with a pleasant and predictable routine. Sadly, the Director died of cancer at the end of his first year, so Len was appointed Acting Director, but without a deputy, so it became rather more demanding. Len held both jobs for two years before the next retiring CAS was appointed over him.

Connie thought it desperately unfair, and Len was thoroughly disgruntled, having proved he could do the job. With the experience of taking on Whitehall over his premature retirement from the British Army, he took his case through the Minister for Civil Defence to the Prime Minister, but was told that the job was more suited to a retired CAS. Harsh words were exchanged. Len resigned, announcing that they were moving to Australia where both their married daughters were living. He and Connie put their savings into a fancy-goods shop in Brisbane. Commerce was not Len's *métier*, however, so they had to sell up at a substantial loss.

They moved to Sydney, where Len became the chief security officer at a factory of Amalgamated Wireless, Australia, a highly respected firm with major defence contacts. For the next ten years Len, in the words of a senior manager, 'Put our security right and kept it there'. Connie became the chief tea-lady of another major Australian firm in the vicinity.

In 1988 both retired, Len without fanfare or fuss; he just went, as he wanted, with no formal farewells. Connie's company would not hear of it. She was invited to the boardroom to sit in the Chairman's chair. There she demurely sipped her tea while the board and senior staff drank her health in something stronger. Coincidentally, April 1988 was their forty-fourth wedding anniversary. The Sydney SAS Assocation sent Connie forty-four red roses. She burst into tears.

They now live in what Australians call a 'relocatable home' at Tweed Heads on the Queensland/New South Wales border. On one side is the Tweed River, on the other the Pacific surf pounds the silver sand.

'Oh, we've had a good life, Len and me. Some oops and downs mind, but now Len has a boat and does a bit o' fishing, and he takes the youngest grandson for long walks. He reckons he'll make the SAS yet.'

NOTES AND SOURCES

Preface

1. See Citation reproduced at Appendix 9.
2. See letter from Sir Horace Clive to his wife, May, 1944, Appendix 7.
3. M.R.D. Foot, *SOE in France*, Annex 'A' (HMSO 1966).

Chapter 1

1. John Willmott (brother) letter to his sister Yvonne Wines dated 16 October, 1987. Appendix 2.
2. Mrs Yvonne Wines (sister), conversations with the author, Melbourne, 30 September, 1987, and subsequently.
3. Army Form B.271 — Attestation Form — Appendix 3
4. Former RSM Bill Weatherly, conversation with the author, Hastings, 17 August, 1988.
5. Died 1985 aged 95.
6. Former RSM Bill Weatherly, conversation with the author 17 August, 1988.

Chapter 2

1. M. R. D. Foot, *SOE 1940–46* (BBC Publications 1984), pp. 11 and 12.
2. Ibid p. 13.
3. Christopher Andrew, *Secret Service* (William Heinemann 1985), p. 533.
4. Sir Douglas Dodds-Parker, letter to the author dated 21 June, 1987.
5. Army Records.
6. 'The Spook Hoose', pointed out to the author when stationed near Crieff in 1947.
7. Joseph Garlinski, *Poland SOE & the Allies* (George Allen & Unwin 1969), pp. 24–26.
8. BBC Broadcast 27 September, 1938.
9. Richard C Lukas, *Forgotten Holocaust* (University Press of Kentucky 1986), p. 89.

Chapter 3

1. Mrs Yvonne Wines, conversation with the author, Melbourne, 30 September, 1987.
2. Army Form B 272, Conduct Sheet, 'Deprived of Lance Stripe' by Major (later Lieutenant-General Sir George) G. C. Gordon-Lennox, Grenadier Guards.
3. M. R. D. Foot, *SOE 1940–46* (BBC Publications 1984), p. 22.
4. SOE Archives.
5. Ibid.
6. M. R. D. Foot, *SOE 1940–46* (BBC Publications 1984). p. 64
7. In fact a charming highlander who rose to be a lieutenant-general and a knight — much amused by Len's description of him.
8. Colonel Harry Cator, Royal Scots Greys, a cousin by marriage of the Queen, and a well-known eccentric.
9. Former RSM Bob Bennett, MM, BEM, one of the 'originals', conversation with the author.
10. Colonel Iain Lapraik DSO OBE MC to the author, November, 1972, Honorary Colonel 21 SAS at the time.
11. Virginia Cowles, *The Phantom Major* (Fontana 1958) p. 22
12. M. R. D. Foot, *SOE in France* (HMSO 1966), p. 79.
13. Colonel Sir David Stirling DSO OBE, White's, 16 September, 1972.
14. Virginia Cowles, *The Phantom Major* (Fontana 1958).
15. SOE archives.

Chapter 4

1. Brigadier E. C. W. Myers CBE DSO, *Greek Entanglement* (Alan Sutton 1985), p. 17.
2. Ibid pp. 14–15.
3. Ibid p. 17.
4. C. M. Woodhouse, *Something Ventured*, (Granada Publishing Ltd 1982), p. 21.
5. *Greek Entanglement* p. 19.
6. Later Lieutenant-General Inder Gill, Indian Army.
7. *Greek Entanglement*, p. 26.
8. Ibid. pp. 49–50.
9. C. M. Woodhouse, letter to the author dated 20 September, 1987.
10. *Greek Entanglement*, p. 52.
11. Ibid p. 57.
12. *Something Ventured*, p. 41.
13. *Greek Entanglement*, p. 69.
14. Ibid p. 71.

15. Ibid p. 74.
16. Ibid p. 78.
17. Ibid p. 79.

Chapter 5

1. Former RSM Bill Weatherly, Royal Signals, conversation with the author, 10 October, 1986.
2. Citation, Army Form W.3121 — see Appendix 4.
3. Brigadier Myers, letter to the author dated 25 September, 1987.
4. See plate 6. Letter Cards from HQ Force 133, M.E.F., to Len's parents, both ref B6/602, dated respectively 24 Jan 44 and 1 Mar 44.
   NOTE: Citation for the BEM was dated 9 Apr 43, awarded 14 Oct 43, letter to Len's parents dated 1 Mar 44. citation for the MM was dated 20 Sep 43, awarded 3 Feb 44 (Immediate), notified to Len's parents 24 Jan 44!
5. *Greek Entanglement*, p. 169.
6. Bill Jordan, *Conquest without Victory*, (Hodder & Stoughton 1969), pp. 43–44.
7. Ibid p. 45.
8. Ibid p. 46.
9. Ibid p. 61.
10. *Greek Entanglement*, p. 94.
11. *Something Ventured*, p. 53.
12. *Greek Entanglement*, p. 95.
13. Jordan, *Conquest without Victory*, p. 66.
14. Ibid p. 67.
15. Ibid p. 44.
16. Former RSM Bill Weatherly, conversation with the author.
17. *Conquest without Victory*, pp. 69–71.
18. Ibid p. 70.
19. Ibid p. 74.
20. Ibid p. 76.
21. *Greek Entanglement*, p. 204.
22. *Something Ventured*, p. 73.

Chapter 6

1. Probably the 'Eureka' set, very secret at the time and designed as a ground beacon to guide planes over the last 15–90 miles to their target. See Diagram, Appendix 5.
2. Army Records, Personal File.

3. Yvonne Wines, conversations with the author.
4. SOE Archives.
5. Sir Douglas Dodds-Parker, letter to the author dated 21 June, 1987.
6. *SOE in France*, p. 408.
7. SOE Archives.
8. Ibid.
9. SOE Archives — After Action Report — Appendix 6.
10. Ibid.
11. Ibid.
12. Ibid.
13. Letter from Sir Horace Clive to his wife in May, 1944. See Appendix 7.

Chapter 7

1. Chester Wilmot, *Struggle for Europe*, (Collins 1952), p. 498.
2. SOE Archives.
3. Ibid.
4. Ibid.
5. Ibid.
6. Ibid.
7. Ibid.
8. Ibid.
9. BUREAU BLJZONDERE OPDRACHTEN No. XI/29 dated 17 Nov 1944. — translation at Appendix 8.
10. Dutch Citation for the Bronze Lion — Appendix 9.
11. Rolls Royce Enthusiasts Club Bulletin No 167 — Apendix 10.
12. General Sir John Jackett, *I Was a Stranger*, (Hogarth Press 1988).

Chapter 8

1. SOE Archives.
2. Army Records.
3. Dr Alex Muirhead, formerly commanding A Squadron 1 SAS, letter to the author, dated 24 May, 1989.
4. The redoubtable Reg Seekings, DCM MM, David Stirling's driver in the desert.
5. Duncan Ridler MM, former Intelligence Sergeant 1 SAS, briefing the author, Westbury-on-Severn, 24 August 1988.

Chapter 9

1. Army Records.
2. Colonel T N Boileau OBE, letter to the author dated 29 November, 1987.

3. Mr Costos Demetrious, restaurateur in Canada, letter to the author dated 26 October, 1989.

Chapter 10

1. Framed on the wall of Director Special Forces Office, London SW3.
2. Tony Geraghty, *Who Dares Wins*, (Fontana paperback 1981), p. 22.
3. Lt Colonel Pat Winter MBE, former Adjutant 22 SAS in Malaya, conversation with the author, June, 1988.
4. The author was an infantry signals officer in Malaya at the same time. Signallers had a rough life.
5. Lt Colonel Pat Winter MBE.
6. *Who Dares Wins*, (Fontana paperback 1981), p. 32.
7. Later Major (QM) Steve Stevenson, SAS Signal Squadron.
8. Major Dare Newell OBE, Regimental Adjutant SAS, letter to the author dated 10 September 1986.
9. Lt Colonel Pat Winter MBE, conversation with the author.
10. Ibid.
11. Ibid.
12. Lt Colonel 'Johnny' Cooper MBE DCM MM, letter to the author.
13. MOD Stanmore letter P/328521/AODO/III/3 — DL 5/4/27, dated 5 May 1970.

APPENDICES

1. Letter from Sir Peter Wilkinson, 15 November, 1987
2. Letter from John Willmott to his sister Yvonne Wines, 16 October, 1987
3. Army Form B.271 — Attestation Form
4. Citation for the British Empire Medal
5. Eureka Ground Beacon
6. After Action Report, 20 September, 1943
7. Letter from Sir Horace Clive to his wife, May, 1944
8. Dutch Report on Arnhem
9. Dutch Citation for the Bronze Lion
10. Rolls Royce Enthusiasts Club Bulletin

15th November, 1087.

Dear Brigadier,

Many thanks for your letter of 21st October about Wilmott.

His description of his War Office interview sounds plausible. In his favour I can confirm that the director of the communications section of the Secret Intelligence Service (SIS) in those days was, surprisingly enough, a former major in the Royal Welch Fusiliers.

Nothing in his description of his training rings obviously false to me, but I have no first-hand experience to go on.

He might well have changed trains at Pilsen (as it was known in German) on his journey from Munich to Prague - after the incorporation of the Sudetenland into the Grossreich in 1938, the German-Czech frontier was only a few miles to the west of Pilsen.

Lowicz is certainly on the direct route from **Prague** to Warsaw, and had he travelled on 30/31st August he might well have got there before War was declared early on the morning of 1st September. And it is conceivable that a young English civilian, speaking no German or Polish, might have been allowed by the Abwehr to travel through the forming-up areas of the German Eighth and Tenth Armies on the eve of the invasion. But only just.

Praga is certainly a suburb of Warsaw (? on the East side of the Vistula).

The British Embassy in Warsaw was (so far as I remember) evacuated during the night 5/6th September, so he would have found nobody there on the 9th, and the British Mission was by then established south of Brest (Brecz-nad-Bugiem) None of the names he mentions is known to me, but I only arrived in Warsaw on 3rd September.

Pace Douglas Dodds-Parker, I am almost certain that no signallers were being recruited by MI6 in 1938 (or in 1939 apart from the signals detachment which accompanied the Polish Mission). But Wilmott's story is (more or less) consistent with his having been recruited by the SIS; which would also account for the Foreign Office's reticence.

His wife's story of his nightmares, to me, lends credence to his story rather than otherwise; I have had similar experiences after World War II and after a tour of duty in Vietnam in 1966.

In short, I cannot fault Wilmott's story, but in your place would want to question him in depth about his movements between 30th August and 9th September. Peter Fleming's YAK Mission was originally a ~~training~~ mission (for recruiting and training Italian POWs). It was given an operational role by Wavell as a stopgap measure (stricto sensu!) at the time of the Greek Campaign. (? does Wilmott claim to have been with P.F.; and if so, was he bombed and sunk with the rest of YAK Mission at Piraeus in the British Embassy yacht; and where did he go from there ? Crete or Alex Cairo or Palestine? He had a long time to fill in before operation HARLING.

Anyhow, he sounds an interesting subject for a biography. *Yours sincerely*
Peter Wilkinson.

151

Dear Yvonne,

Thank you for your letter which we received just a few days ago. Sorry that I cannot give you any further news about Arthur as we have not heard from Betty since 5th September although we have written twice to her. Either she cannot find time to write letters or she is unable to sit down by herself and write what she wishes.

We were interested to learn that someone is looking into Len's background with the object of writing a book about him, although after all this time, wartime exploits are somewhat out of date. It will be good though to have some record of the things which he did.

There is no doubt that, if I drew on my memory, I could relate a number of things about Len when he was a boy. I can remember his going into the army and the things which he talked about when he came home on leave. I can well remember the time when he was in one of the Military Tattoos as a toy soldier, then another one when he was a motorcycle rider in the Signal Corps. He always was somewhat daring in his younger days and it was very likely for that reason the he became a paratrooper as soon as war broke out, maybe even before.

You ask about Dad and his background. I am afraid that the truth about him died with Mum, if she ever new the full truth. I recall many times asking him about his background and never getting very far. He did adnmit to me that his family name was McRae but neither he nor Mum would ever really explain why, and when he changed his name. There was some deep secret there which neither would ever reveal. There have been various stories over the years, such as the fact that he changed his name because his family had stolen all his money and he wanted to get away from them completely, but this was always hard to believe. He did reckon that he had spent a number of years in India driving steam engines but there was little proof of this, although he seemed to know a bit about India. He did let slip once, that he had served in the army in India but once again this was never enlarged upon. His whole background was a secret, including his age, as he was apparently older than he claimed to be. This was discovered when he died and Mum tried to claim on some insurance policies. Whoever, and whatever he was, he was definitely an educated man, taking into account the standards of education which would have pertained when he was a boy. I do think, however, that he must have been somewhat adventurous himself, and this possibly reflected in Len. Who knows?

As for Mum, well she told us so many different stories that it was hard to separate truth from fantasy. As you well know, she would have nothing to do with her sisters Bertha and Annie and as a result I grew up without knowing them. After Mum died Annie wrote to us to try to make contact and I took that opportunity to write back to her to try and find out some background to her and Dad. Unfortunately, by the time that I had written back to her she had died and any information, which she would have had, died with her. Arthur's son, Michael, has also expressed an interest in his grandparents and when we were in England I gave him as much information as possible, as he is going to try and go backwards to see if he can unearth anything. I doubt that he will because I feel that the tracks have been covered too well and the trail is too cold to find out any pertinent facts. Dad was born in the days that birth certificates were not required and although he said that he was born in Dumfries, where would any records be kept, even if there were any, and who can be sure that Dumfries is where he was born?

You commented about our cyclone, well it wasn't a cyclone but a tornado. It took the roofs off about twenty houses but as it was only about twenty metres wide we hardly knew anything about it. As for living in Whakatane, it is a lovely place to live, lovely climate, quiet and peaceful. Earthquakes do not worry us, they are a way of life and we have to get used to them. At least we do not have bush fires.

Description of _Rowan Richard_ ~~Inglis~~ _Wimott_ on Enlistment.

Apparent Age........_15_....years...............months.

(To be determined by examining Medical Officer and based on physical development according to the instructions given in the Regulations for Army Medical Services.)

Height......................_4_.ft _8¾_.ins.

Weight ...._____73_.lbs.

Chest measurement { Girth when fully expanded ....} ...._29_.ins.

{ Range of expansion } ...._3_.ins.

Complexion ...._Fresh_

Eyes ...._Grey_

Hair ...._Brown_

Religious Denomination*._Roman Catholic_

* Precise denomination to be entered, viz., Church of England, Presbyterian (including Church of Scotland, United Free Church of Scotland, Free Church of Scotland, Presbyterian Church of England, Presbyterian Church in Ireland, and Presbyterian Church of Wales or the Calvinistic Methodist Church of Wales), Roman Catholic, Methodist (including Wesleyan, Primitive Methodist or United Methodist), †Baptist, †Congregationalist, Jewish or other denomination stated by the recruit.
† Comprising the United Army Board.

Distinctive marks and marks indicating congenital peculiarities or previous disease.

(Should the Medical Officer be of opinion that the recruit has served before, he will, unless the man acknowledges to any previous service, attach a slip to that effect, for the information of the Approving Officer.)

scar onter side of right eye

In the case of boys educated at Duke of York's, Royal Military School, Queen Victoria School, or Industrial or Reformatory School (under Home Office, etc.), state school.

School..

....

Certificate of Primary Military Examination.

I hereby certify that the above-named recruit was inspected by me and I consider him *.........._fit_.....for service in the†...._Royal Corps of Signals_.....and that due care has been exercised in his enlistment. I also certify that Question 17 ~~18~~ of the attestation on page 1 has been suitably completed to meet the requirements for the period for which he has enlisted or re-enlisted.

Date ...._1 July_....., 19_36_ ...._H F Nash_ _Majr_ } Recruiting Officer.

Place ...._Brighton_.... ....

* Insert here " fit " or " unfit." † Insert the " Regiment " or " Corps."

Certificate of Medical Examination.

I have examined the above-named recruit in accordance with the instructions laid down in the Regulations for Army Medical Services and consider him*...._fit_..............for the Army.

Date ...._1 July_...., 19_36_ ...._J. J. Wynn_ _Lieut Col_ _Rank_

Place ...._Brighton_.... ....
* Insert here " fit " or " unfit." _Medical Officer._

NOTE.—Should the Medical Officer consider the Recruit unfit, he will fill in the foregoing Certificate only in the case of those who have been attested, and will briefly state below the cause of unfitness :—

....

....

....

....

*Certificate of Approving Officer.

I certify that this Attestation of the above-named recruit is correct, and properly filled up, and that the required forms appear to have been complied with. I accordingly approve, and appoint him to the†...._Royal Corps of Signals_.....

If enlisted by special authority, Army Form B. 203 (or other authority for the enlistment) will be attached to the _original and duplicate_ attestations.

Date ...._1 July_........., 19_36_ ...._H F Nash_ _Majr_ } Approving Officer.

Place ...._Brighton_.... ....

* The signature of the Approving Officer is to be affixed in the presence of the Recruit.
† Here insert the " Corps " for which the Recruit has been enlisted.

Army Form
W. 3121.

Date Recommendation passed forward.

Received

Passed

Brigade _____
Division _____
Corps _____
Army _____

Brigade _____ Division _____ Corps _____

MOST SECRET

Unit	Regtl. No.	Rank and Name (Christian names must be stated)	Action for which commended (Date and place of action must be stated)	Recommended by	Honour or Reward	(To be left blank)
R.Sigs.	2552304	Sigmn (L/Cpl) WILLMOTT Howard Richard Douglas	This N.C.O. volunteered for special duties operating into Greece on the night of 30 Sep 42 ...	M.O.4.	B.E.M.	

Immediate Award

N1c

Awarded B.E.M.
AG 14 10.43

General,
Commander-in-Chief,
Middle East Forces.

Head of Mission

9th Apr 43

153 56

After taxiing down the runway, the plane came to a stop, facing into the wind next to the agent's light. The engines did not stop turning, and the crew members stayed at their posts. Each member of the "reception committee" played a very precise role. Underground fighters guarded the area. At the left, the man kneeling is disassembling the secret "Eurêka" ground beacon which has controlled the plane over the last 90 to 15 miles and has automatically guided it into the axis of the field. Once folded up, the Eurêka, its power supply, and its aerial were placed in a small carrying case that protected it from dirt.

The agent wearing a topcoat conceals the S-Phone, whose aerial is visible. With it, he can communicate with the pilot or any crew member for 20 to 5 minutes before the plane appears, depending on its altitude. Likewise, after takeoff, and under the same conditions, the ground agent can give his final oral instructions to the departed agents. This instrument is virtually undetectable.

© 1972 by Pierre Lorain

155

Army Form V

Date recommendati
passed forward

	Received	Passed
Brigade		
Division		
Corps		
Army GHQ · 20 504 143		

_____ Brigade _____ Division _____ Corps

Schedule No. _____
(To be left blank)

Unit. R. Sigs. _____

Rank and Army or Personal No. WS/Sjt.   2325304.

Name WILLMOTT, Leonard Richard Douglas.
(Christian names must be stated)

MOST SECRET

Action for which commended (Date and place of action must be stated)	Recommended by	Honour or Reward	(To be left blank)

On 30 May, 43, instructions were sent to Brig. MYERS to arrange for the cutting of all the main North to South communications in GREECE, between the end of June and the first week of July.

Plans had already been prepared for this eventuality and Brig. MYERS issued instructions for all the main roads and the railway and all telephone lines to be cut on 21 Jun. 43, and to be kept cut by further demolitions up to 7 Jul. with a view to making them unusable for a further seven days, i.e., up to 14 Jul. This series of operations was known as Operation "ANIMALS".

During the period 21 Jun. to 10 Jul. the British personnel of Brig. MYERS' Mission were employed night after night on different operations throughout GREECE, cutting the roads and the railway.   Owing to the greater reliability of British personnel, only a small proportion of the total Andarti strength was made use of.   The success of Operation "ANIMALS" was due to the magnificent way in which the British personnel acted under the command of the four senior Liaison Officers under whom Brig. MYERS had decentralised responsibility for areas throughout GREECE.

Throughout "ANIMALS" operations the work of Brig. MYERS' wireless personnel often passed unnoticed.   Under active service conditions - and most trying ones at that - often in danger, Sjt. WILLMOTT's work was of the very highest order.

.... During the past two months Sjt. WILLMOTT's Station has been repeatedly bombed by the enemy.   His personal courage and devotion to duty have been exemplary throughout the most trying and dangerous conditions.

On at least two occasions Sjt. WILLMOTT has continued to operate his set whilst actually being bombed.

Recommended by: M.O.4.

Honour or Reward: M.M. (Immediate).

General
Commander-in-Chief
Middle East Forces

18025

Awarded M.M
LG. 3-2-44

Brig.

20 Sep. 43.

Red Rice
    Andover
        Hants.

Beloved,

Would that you'd been at home this morn, for just after I'd closed my letter to you the bell rang and a young sergt. of R.C. of Signals with the M.M., B.E.M. and Desert Medal asked if we knew Jim Russell. I took him into the drawing room and the moment he saw the H. Coster photo of N, he said, 'That's Jim Russell', N's official name in Greece. Then he talked for nearly 2 hours till I had to go to Waterloo.

I made copious notes and will make the best story I can with my shaky hand:-

N was parachuted out on Nov 12 on the west coast of Greece near Tsaritsena and worked first under and then over this chap Len Willmott. They all have a name given to them and N is 'Jim Russell'. They're living in squalid Greek hotels in the mountains, up to 10,000 feet, and change houses every week or 10 days. N now speaks excellent mountain Greek, quite different from the town Greek, generally wears battledress in case he sh'd be caught, in the hope that he'd be treated as a prisoner of war, a faint hope, for 4 have been caught in the last 18 months and all were shot. N's job is intelligence and collecting all information of German movements, military, civilian, stores, equipment, etc, etc. This is then coded by him and his (not over-trustworthy) Greek wireless telegraphists and pushed thro' to Cairo. (Incidentally Len knows who [name crossed out] is, but not under that name.) N gets his dope from an army of scouts on the roads, who are all paid in gold, which, with all required stores, ammunition and equipment, is dropped from planes. 60 Halifaxes a month go to Greece from Egypt. All stuff going out from Greece goes by submarine, caique or tiny sloop.

They live mainly on cornbread, goat's meat and haricot beans, but eggs, sugar, coffee and Pilsner beer can be bought for them in the towns by friendly runners. Very short of smokes, only a v. coarse local tobacco folded in a sort of cabbage leaf. So I've immediately sent word to Moorgate to send 1000 Players monthly to ISLD as Len says they're certain to reach him. They drink a lot of lovely clean spring water; quite a little is a grand thirst-quencher. N's first 3 months in the mountains brought him, like all newcomers, a lot of mountain fever and jaundice, but he's grandly fit now — or was on March 15 when Len left by sub for Bari, whence he flew to Cairo. The one great trouble is lice, as big as bugs, and you never get your clothes off.

Well, that's about all on dear old N, except that he's fatter than in the Coster photo and very broad and strong. Len reached England Easter

Monday and has since been lecturing all over England to prospective recruits for ISLD. He's on leave in London till June 30, has a flat in Harlesden with a young wife, but probably wont leave England till mid-July when he leaves in plain clothes with a French Mayor for ??? (sic). If he finds himself anywhere near London in early July he'll ring up so as to come up and see you.

He's only 23, has 9 yrs' service, of which the last 6 in ISLD. He was in Germany Sept '39, went into Poland, then went to France and eventually found the easiest way to return to England was thro' Germany!!! with an American passport.

Doesn't it all sound like a fairy tale? But oh how fascinating. If you'd like to write to him the address is Len Willmott, 173 Holland Road, Harlesden, N.W. 10.

There's no secret about N being in Greece but keep all else that I've written under your hat; their chief work is information and sabotage.

[The letter concludes with matters of purely family interest.]

DUTCH REPORT ON ARNHEM.

BUREAU BLJZCNDERE OPDRACHTEN (SPECIAL OPERATIONS)
NO.XI/29   17th November 1944.

SECRET

From: Major General J W van Ooschat
Chief of Bureau B.O.

Addressed to: His Excellency The Minister of War

In connection with the recent telephone conversations with Captain van der Reidt, I reconsidered the proposals made by me in my letters of 10 Oct 1944 No X/16 and 21 Oct 44 No X/34 and examined material thoroughly once more. The result of certain points has given me cause, Your Excellency, to inform you of the following.

Captain Staal has distinguished himself together with Captain McCord Sollenberger, 2nd Lt L R D Willmott and Sergeant J Billingsley immediately on arrival in the Netherlands by great action and demonstration of courage and diligence. As an example I inform you about the performance of Captain Staal and Captain Sollenberger. They were landed in the vicinity of Groesbeek. Both officers at that particular moment went on their own from Groesbeek to Malden so as to make contact with the Dutch Resistance Group. They crossed the woods with great care where it turned out later 400 of the enemy were lurking, and organised the Resistance so efficiently that our troops that arrived later benefited greatly.

Later Captain Staal started an Information Bureau in Nijmegen where he made direct telephone communication with the Resistance In Arnhem, Utrecht, Rotterdam Amsterdam, the Hague and Gouda. To achieve these communications demanded great cunning and caution. The result obtained by Staal proved of great importance to the Allies who arrived later. 21st Army Group, HQ 30 Corps, and until now benefited from this information.

Captain Staal has performed first class work under extremely difficult circumstances. When the airborne troops arrived in Nijmegen they experienced a desperate shortage of means of transport.

Captain Sollenberger decided to go on his own through enemy occupied Nijmegen. He penetrated through the sentries and succeeded to enter the town and to go into a garage, where he found two cars which had been made inoperable. With the assistance of members of the Resistance in Nijmegen he made the cars workable and transported the cars to his own troops, where they were a welcome asset.

Captain Staal and Captain Sollenberger wanted to establish contact after their arrival in Nijmegen with the Resistance in Arnhem. As this did not succeed, they went over the bridge from Nijmegen to Arnhem. Via roundabout routes they arrived in Driel; straight through the enemy occupation, and in Driel they managed to make contact with the Polish Parachutists who were already there.

Crossing the river in DUKWS they came in contact in Arnhem with the Allied 1st Airborne Division that was there, and supplied important information about the organisation and the developments of the operations. During the whole journey and by the fact of crossing the river in boats, they were under very heavy artillery fire.

The 2nd Lieutenant Willmott and Sergeant Billingsley served as radio operators in the department of Captain Staal. They had constantly to clean their transmission sets from the sand and dirt which explosions caused. Without interruptions they remained always in action. Their transmission was excellent both in sending and receiving in which is included decoding of messages in code.

Their service did not give them the opportunity to carry out noticeable heroic achievements but Captain Staal reported that in carrying out their orders they conducted themselves in an heroic manner.

After the landing they had two hours for each operator to contact London; and indeed they kept the communication going night and day without interruptions; in the trenches and shelters under the constant mortar and grenade fire. Without interruption, they remained always in action.

Their transmission was excellent, both in sending and receiving, in which is included decoding of messsages in code. Captain Staal is of the opinion that both these radio operators 'have achieved the impossible.'

The 1st Lieutenant M J Knottenbelt arrived with the 1st Airborne troops in Arnhem and let himself down with a parachute although he had never even used one before. This on its own was quite an achievement.

He started after the landing immediately with the organisation of the Resistance and did this in an excellent manner. He assassinated a German General. Although he was seriously wounded by a mortar projectile he continued his task and swam wounded across the Rhine. When he returned to Nijmegen he was taken to hospital in an exhausted state. He had achieved from the start useful work.

Captain A J Bestenbreutge has, as a parachutist, organised the army of the Resistance at Nijmegen. These Resistance Groups gave valuable support to the Allied troops. A reconnaissance journey in Nijmegen, Bestenbreutge came under machine-gun fire and had four shots in the left arm and one in the left hand. Notwithstanding this he continued his reconnaissance until his mission was completed.

I believe from all this it is reasonable to reach the conclusion that Staal,

Sollenberger, Willmot and Besebreutge should be recommended to receive the Bronze Cross.

The Major Wilson, Lieutenant Verhaeghe, Sergeant Benyobn, Lieutenant Dubois, Lieutenant Faben and Sergeant Mason formed part of the Netherlands Mission belonging to the Arnhem Troop which took part in operations in the vicinity of Nijmegen and Arnhem.

They all performed their duty in a splendid way, but were not in a position to be in the limelight. Notwithstanding, I am of the opinion that they should be considered to receive a token of consideration also on the grounds of motivation concerning foreigners, which I brought to attention in my letter of 19th October 1944, No X/16. The token of appreciation would be the granting of the Service Cross.

Signed

J W van Ooschat
The General Major, Bureau B.O.

Addressed to: His Excellency The Minister of War

No. 20

We Wilhelmina, by the grace of God.
Queen of the Netherlands, Princess of
Orange—Nassau, etc., etc., etc.

On the recommendation of Our Ministers of War and for Foreign Affairs:

HAVE APPROVED AND ORDERED:

To award the BRONZE LION to:

Second Lieutenant L. R. D. W I L L M O T T ,
British Army,

for:

"Exceptional gallantry, leadership, ability and tenacity
of purpose, displayed during the operations of the First
Airborne Division near Arnhem in September 1944; after
landing in enemy-occupied territory, he fulfilled his task
in an excellent manner."

Our Ministers of War and for Foreign Affairs are, each for his own part,
in charge of the execution of this Decree.

Het Loo   ,   5th September 1946

(sgd.) WILHELMINA.

The Minister of War,
(sgd.) A.H.J.L.FIEVEZ.

The Minister for Foreign Affairs,
(sgd.) Mr. C.G.W.H. BARON VAN
 BOETZELAER VAN OOST RHOUT.

For true copy, true extract, and true translation,

The Secretary-General of the Ministry of War,

No. 262d
Ⓐ 14380 - '45 - K 983

162

BULLETIN 167

THE GERMAN GENERAL'S BENTLEY

The comment in the Bulletin calls to mind an incident concerning a Bentley.
Before the war a Dutchman bought a three and a half litre Bentley, which he
had serviced at Derby.   He was an enthusiastic owner and sought permission
from the Company to bring a camera into the works to photograph his car and
the parts that had been removed from it.   He was an engaging character and
as a result of his request he was allowed into No.6 shop, which was the
service station,with his camera.   He took a number of photographs and nothing
more was thought of it.   In 1940, during the German attack on the Low Countries,
he turned out to be a German collaborator.

Having been through Stanley Sedgwick's book on all the Bentleys, I came across
a name that rang a bell,Th. Van Marken of Baarn, who bought B-23-FC, fitted
with a Vanden Plas touring body.   The dates line up with what is known of
the visits to the works mentioned above.   It seems to me that B-23-FC and
Mr Van Marken meet the case, because the name seems familiar and the story
was confirmed to me by separate sources I could trust.   It could well be
that B-23-FC, which was owned postwar by Dr A.J.Van Eunen of Haarlem and
later Sqn/Ldr W.H. Armstrong in Germany, could have been the General's car.
It will be understood that the name was based on memory and could be doing
someone an injustice, but the incident shows how well the enemy was organised.

BIBLIOGRAPHY

M. R. D. Foot, *SOE in Europe* (Official History) HMSO, 1966.

M. R. D. Foot, *SOE 1940–46*, BBC Publications 1984.

Winston Churchill, *The Second World War* — Volumes I and VI, Cassel & Co 1947 and 1954.

F. H. Hinkley, *British Intelligence in World War II*, HMSO, 1984.

Christopher Andrew, *Secret Service*, William Heinemann, 1985.

Anthony Cavendish, *Inside Intelligence*, William Collins, 1987.

Nigel West, *GCHQ*, Weidenfeld & Nicolson 1986.

Lt General Sir Adrian Carton de Wiart, *Happy Odyssey*, Jonathan Cape, 1950.

Joseph Garlinski, *Poland, SOE and the Allies*, George Allen & Unwin 1969.

Richard Lukas, *The Forgotten Holocaust*, University of Kentucky Press 1986.

Kenneth Macksey, *Partisans of Europe*

Brigadier E. C. W. Myers, *Greek Entanglement*, Alan Sutton, 1985.

C. M. Woodhouse, *The Struggle for Greece*

C. M. Woodhouse, *Something Ventured*, Granada Publishing, 1982.

William Jordan, *Conquest Without Victory*, Hodder & Stoughton, 1969.

Nigel Clive, *A Greek Experience*, Michael Russell, 1985.

Chester Wilmot, *The Struggle for Europe*, Collins, 1952.

Marcel Ruby, *F Section SOE*, Leo Cooper, 1988.

Philippe Garnier-Raymond, *The Tangled Web*, Arthur Barker Ltd, 1968.

M. R. D. Foot (Edited by) *Holland at War against Hitler*, Frank Cass, 1990.

General Sir John Hackett, *I was a Stranger*, Hogarth Press, 1988.

Virginia Cowles, *The Phantom Major*, Collins, 1958.

Tony Geraghty, *Who Dares Wins*, Little Brown & Co 1980.

INDEX

Metzovo Pass, 79
MI 6(D), 16
MI 6(R), 16, 22
MI 6, 14, 89, 117, 120, 121
Michalli, 62, 64, 70
MM, vxiii, 3, 6, 67, 80, 83, 134, 138
MO 1 (SP), 34, 110
Montgomery, General Sir Bernard, 48
MPAJA (Malayan People's Anti-Japanese Army), 127
Mt Carmel, x, 45
Mt Giona, 48, 50, 52, 58
Mt Oiti, 59, 63
Muirhead, Captain Alex, MC, 112
Munich, 22, 23
Mur de Bretagne, 84, 88, 90
Myers, Colonel (later Brigadier) ECW, CBE DSO, x, 48, 51, 52, 54–59, 61–66, 68, 70–81, 83, 97, 98

Nash, Major HE, 8
Netherlands Bronze Lion, xvii, 98, 134
Netherlands Resistance Cross, xvii, 98, 134
New Zealanders, x, 51, 68, 133, 136
Newall, Major Dare, OBE, 127, 131–134
Newhaven, 4
Nicholls, Brigadier FW, 14
NID (Q), 34
Nijmegen, 84, 96–98
Nolan, Sergeant Tom, 36, 44, 47

OBE, 67, 81
OCTU, 118
Olympus, 74
Oosterbeek, 98
Otterfing, 23
Oudenhoof, 98
Owens, Sergeant 'Taffy', 83–84, 85

Palmer, Captain Peter, 43
Papadia, 48, 50, 58
Parga, 68, 70
Paris, 21–22, 85–86
'Passy', Colonel (Colonel A Dewarvrin DSO MC) pp. 83, 88, 90
'Patch', 83, 85
Patton, General 'Blood & Guts', 88
Peleponnese, 72
Phillips, Sergeant Doug, x, 50, 51, 60, 68, 70, 72, 77
Pickfords, 19
pig, Master Cook's, 45–46
Pilsen, 24
Pindus Mountains, 79
Pistolis, Yani, 58, 59, 68
Poland, 22, 23, 86
Polish Resistance, 27

Praga, 27
Prague, 24
Princess Royal, HRH The, 12
Prophet Elias, 55, 56

Ranjituri, SS, 136
Ranzau, Sergeant 'Red', 36, 44
RCB (Regular Commissions Board), 111
Reading Airfield, 21
Rennes, 85
Reprisals, 29
Resistance, 87
Rhine, River, 92, 97
Ridler, Sergeant Duncan, MM, 113
Roumeli, 72
Rudellat, Yvonne ('Jacquline')
Rustum Buildings, 36, 43, 44
RWF (Royal Welsh Fusiliers) pp. 16, 20, 21

Sabotage, 29
Sakai, 127
Salmon, Major John, 132
SAS (Special Air Service), 35, 37, 38, 41, 44, 50, 73, 87, 88, 109, 111, 112, 113, 125, 126, 129, 130, 133
SAS, 21st (Artists Rifles), 127
SAS, 22nd, 127, 132
Savona Bomber, 78
Schoofs, Captain Herman Andre MBE, 88, 91
Shepheards Hotel, 47
Simpson, Brigadier John, CBE, ix, x
SIS (Secret Intelligence Service), 16, 23, 87
SIS (Section VIII (Communications), 16, 18
Skolikaria, 74, 75
Slim, Captain the Hon. John (now Colonel the Viscount, OBE), 133
Sloane, Lt Colonel 'Tod' (later Major General), 129, 132
'Smirnoff', Colonel KGB, 139, 140
Smith, Warrant Officer Stan, 74, 75
SOE (Cairo), 46, 48, 71
SOE (Special Operations Executive), ix, x, xvii, xviii, 16, 34, 35, 43, 76, 82, 83, 101, 111, 117, 127
Sollenburger, Captain McCord, 94, 95
Soviet Zone of Germany, 121, 122
Spain, 31
St Briac, 90
St Michel-en-Grève, 91
St Nazarre, 87
Staal, Captain Jacob, 94, 95, 96, 97, 98, 99, 100
Stevenson, Sergeant 'Steve', 131
Stevens, Colonel, 88, 91
Stirling, Captain (later Colonel Sir David,